Passwords

Social Studies Vocabulary

United States History: The Constitution to 1920

CURRICULUM ASSOCIATES®, INC.

To the Student

What is **federalism**? How are a **monopoly** and a **monarchy** the same? What does an **abolitionist** believe? *Passwords: Social Studies Vocabulary* will help you learn the words you need to do well in social studies.

Each lesson in this book is about a different topic in United States history. Every lesson focuses on ten words that will help you understand the topic. The lessons include a reading selection that uses all ten vocabulary words. Four practice activities follow the reading selection. Using each vocabulary word many times will help you remember the word and its meaning. A writing activity ends the lesson. You will use the vocabulary words you have learned to write an eyewitness account, a narrative, an informational article, or a description.

If you need help with a vocabulary word as you do the activities, use the Glossary at the back of the book. The Glossary defines each word and shows you the correct way to pronounce the word. It also has pictures to help you understand the meaning of difficult words.

As you work on the lessons, you may learn other new words besides the vocabulary words. Keep track of those other words in My Social Studies Vocabulary on pages 94–98.

Turn to pages 99 and 100 to learn about roots, prefixes, and suffixes. Find out how they can help you understand new words.

ISBN 978-0-7609-4707-4
©2008—Curriculum Associates, Inc.
North Billerica, MA 01862
No part of this book may be reproduced by any means
without written permission from the publisher.
All Rights Reserved. Printed in USA.
15 14 13 12 11 10 9 8 7 6 5 4 3 2 1

Table of Contents

LESSON 1

colony	Great Awakening	political	revolution	rights
preach	authority	independence	declaration	clause

Religion has played an important part in American history. Some of the first English settlers came to America because of their beliefs. Read this selection to learn about another time when religion changed history.

The Break from Great Britain

The Great Awakening

In the early 1600s everyone in England was expected to join the Church of England. Some people were not happy with the church's rules. They left England. Many came to North America. Some settled in colonies in New England. A **colony** is an area ruled by another country. Over time, however, religion became less important to people in the colonies.

Then, in the 1730s, people became interested in religion again. Men like Jonathan Edwards began to **preach**, or talk about religious subjects, in an exciting way. New churches with new ideas sprang up. This time is known as the **Great Awakening**.

Colonists developed new religious ideas. They put less trust in religious authority.

People returned to church during the Great Awakening.

Authority is official power. Soon, they put less trust in political authority. **Political** means having to do with the government. The Great Awakening helped bring about the American Revolution.

The Declaration of Independence and the American Revolution

By 1770, many colonists wanted **independence**, or freedom, from Great Britain. In 1775, battles broke out between the colonists and British soldiers. The American Revolution had begun. A **revolution** is a war against one's own government.

In 1776, Thomas Jefferson and other leaders met in Philadelphia. They wanted to declare their freedom from Great Britain. Jefferson wrote a **declaration**, a serious statement about something. In the Declaration of Independence, Jefferson wrote that all people are born with rights. **Rights** are freedoms that are protected by law. The Declaration of Independence states that government should protect these rights.

Jefferson also included a **clause**, or section, ending the slave trade. Some people refused to approve this clause. Jefferson was forced to remove it. On July 4, 1776, the Declaration of Independence was approved. The colonies stated that they were free. Their war for freedom would last seven more years.

In 1783, the American Revolution ended. The United States of America was a free country. It was now time to form a new government.

British soldiers fired on an angry crowd in Boston in 1770.

The Declaration of Independence says that all men are created equal.

My Social Studies Vocabulary

Go to page 94 to list other words you have learned about the break from Great Britain.

colony	Great Awakening	political	revolution	rights
preach	authority	independence	declaration	clause

A. *Fill in the blanks with the correct vocabulary word.*

1. a section of a document

   — — — — — —

2. a war against one's own government

   — — — — — — — — — —

3. an area ruled by another country

   — — — — — —

4. a serious statement about something

   — — — — — — — — — — —

5. having to do with the government

   — — — — — — — — —

6. freedoms that are protected by law

   — — — — — —

7. freedom from control

   — — — — — — — — — — — —

8. a period of renewed interest in religion

   — — — — —   — — — — — — — —

9. to talk about religious subjects

   — — — — — —

10. official power

    — — — — — — — — —

B. *Circle the word that makes sense in each sentence. Then write the word.*

1. To gain (clause, independence) from Great Britain, the colonies went to war.

   _____

2. Freedom of religion and freedom to speak are two important (colony, rights).

   _____

3. An area ruled by another country is a (clause, colony).

   _____

4. A church is a place you might hear someone (Great Awakening, preach).

   _____

5. One section, or (clause, authority), was left out. _____

6. The time of renewed interest in religion in the 1730s is called the

   (Great Awakening, revolution). _____

7. During difficult times, people in a country may lose trust in their (authority, political) leaders. _____

8. The writer was very careful in creating his (revolution, declaration).

   _____

9. She is a leader with a position of (authority, colony) in the community.

   _____

10. A new nation might be created by a (independence, revolution).

    _____

WORD ROOT

The word **revolution** comes from the Latin word **revolutio**, which means "turn."

| colony | Great Awakening | political | revolution | rights |
| preach | authority | independence | declaration | clause |

C. *Choose the correct vocabulary word to complete each sentence.*

1. People became interested in religion again when they heard Jonathan Edwards
   _____ .

2. For many years, Virginia was a _____ under the rule
   of Great Britain.

3. The legal paper had a _____ , or section, that no one
   understood.

4. A government should protect the _____ of the people.

5. We choose _____ leaders in elections.

6. New churches were formed during the _____
   of the 1730s.

7. Choose your words carefully when you write a _____ .

8. When people in positions of _____ speak,
   you should listen.

9. Americans fought for their _____ from Great Britain.

10. Many soldiers died in the long and bloody _____ .

colony	Great Awakening	political	revolution	rights
preach	authority	independence	declaration	clause

D. *Use each pair of words in a sentence.*

1. colony, independence

   _____

   _____

   _____

2. preach, Great Awakening

   _____

   _____

   _____

3. declaration, clause

   _____

   _____

   _____

4. authority, political

   _____

   _____

   _____

5. revolution, rights

   _____

   _____

   _____

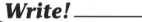

Write! _____

Write your response to the prompt on a separate sheet of paper.
Use as many vocabulary words as you can in your writing.

How did religion help shape American history in the early years
of our country?

constitution   Magna Carta   document   taxation   pilgrim

foundation   parliament   subject   monarchy   compact

A strong plant needs strong roots. A strong government needs strong roots too. What were the roots, or beginnings, of American government? Read this selection to find out.

The Roots of the Constitution

A **constitution** is a set of laws and ideas that describe how a government works. The United States Constitution describes the government of the United States. The United States Constitution was written in 1787. The foundation of our Constitution is much older. A **foundation** is the base upon which something is built. What forms the foundation of the Constitution?

The Magna Carta

In 1215 in England, a group of nobles met and wrote the Magna Carta. The **Magna Carta** is a list of political rights. Political rights are rights that have to do with the government. The Magna Carta set up a **parliament**, a group of people chosen to make laws. The English nobles forced the king to agree to it. The Magna Carta limited the power of the king.

King John is forced to agree to the Magna Carta.

The Roots of the Constitution

The English Bill of Rights

In 1689, another historic **document**, or formal piece of writing, was created in England. This document is known as the Bill of Rights. In the English Bill of Rights, the king and queen of England agreed that they were **subject** to law. That means that the king and queen had to follow the laws that Parliament passed.

The English Bill of Rights also gave Parliament the right of taxation. **Taxation** is the system of paying taxes, or money paid to support the government. The English Bill of Rights limited the power of the monarchy. In a **monarchy**, a country is ruled by one person, such as a king or queen.

King William III and Queen Mary II are shown holding the English Bill of Rights.

The Mayflower Compact

Another document that shaped the Constitution was written in the Atlantic Ocean! In 1620, a group of people set sail across the Atlantic Ocean. The name of their ship was the *Mayflower*. They planned to start a new colony in North America. They called themselves the Pilgrims. A **pilgrim** is a person who makes a long trip for religious reasons. The Pilgrims came to America looking for religious freedom.

Before they landed, the Pilgrims wrote a plan for government. They called their plan the Mayflower Compact. A **compact** is an agreement. In the Mayflower Compact, the Pilgrims agreed to make laws for the good of the community. They also agreed to obey the laws of the colony.

A Pilgrim signs the Mayflower Compact.

My Social Studies Vocabulary

Go to page 94 to list other words you have learned about the roots of the Constitution.

constitution   Magna Carta   document   taxation   pilgrim
foundation   parliament   subject   monarchy   compact

A. *Match each word with its meaning. Write the letter of the correct meaning on the line in front of each word.*

1. _____ taxation

2. _____ compact

3. _____ Magna Carta

4. _____ constitution

5. _____ subject

6. _____ pilgrim

7. _____ foundation

8. _____ document

9. _____ parliament

10. _____ monarchy

a. a group of people chosen to make laws

b. a set of laws and ideas that describe a government

c. a list of political rights created by English nobles in 1215

d. rule by one person, such as a king or queen

e. a formal piece of writing

f. under the power of another

g. an agreement

h. a person who travels a long distance for religious reasons

i. the act of raising money to support the government

j. the base upon which something is built

The Roots of the Constitution

constitution	Magna Carta	document	taxation	pilgrim
foundation	parliament	subject	monarchy	compact

B. *Circle the word that makes sense in each sentence. Then write the word.*

1. A person who makes a long trip for a religious reason is a (compact, pilgrim).

   _____

2. A form of government headed by a king or queen is a (monarchy, parliament).

   _____

3. A country with a written plan of government has a (taxation, constitution).

   _____

4. When you are in school, you are (pilgrim, subject) to the rules of the school.

   _____

5. Before they landed, the Pilgrims wrote a (taxation, compact), or agreement, about how they would be governed. _____

6. The government has the right to raise money through (taxation, foundation).

   _____

7. English nobles forced the king to sign the (Magna Carta, parliament).

   _____

8. A group of people chosen to make laws is a (constitution, parliament).

   _____

9. You need a strong and solid (Magna Carta, foundation) to build a government.

   _____

10. The English Bill of Rights is an important historical (constitution, document).

   _____

WORD ROOT

The word **monarchy** has its root in the Greek word **monos**, which means "alone."

| constitution | Magna Carta | document | taxation | pilgrim |
| foundation | parliament | subject | monarchy | compact |

C. *Write the vocabulary word that best completes each pair of sentences.*

1. After the long trip, the _____ entered the church to pray.

   The holy city welcomed each _____ .

2. Some countries have a government, but do not have a _____ .

   A written plan for government is called a _____ .

3. The people who live in a country are _____ to its laws.

   Even kings and queens are _____ to the law.

4. A formal piece of writing is a _____ .

   A report card is an example of a _____ .

5. English nobles met with the king and made him sign the _____ .

   The power of the king was limited by the _____ .

6. According to our _____ , I wash the dishes and my brother
   dries them.

   Two nations may sign a _____ , or agreement to help
   each other.

7. For many years, the country was a _____ , ruled by a king.

   The power of a king or queen can be limited, even in a _____ .

8. It is difficult to build a nation without a solid _____ .

   Like a building, a country needs a _____ to build upon.

9. Countries raise money through _____ .

   Governments need _____ to pay for school and roads.

10. Laws are passed in the _____ .

    How are members of _____ chosen?

constitution	Magna Carta	document	taxation	pilgrim
foundation	parliament	subject	monarchy	compact

D. *Use each word in a sentence that shows you understand the meaning of the word.*

1. document _____

_____

2. constitution _____

_____

3. pilgrim _____

_____

4. subject _____

_____

5. foundation _____

_____

6. compact _____

_____

7. parliament _____

_____

8. taxation _____

_____

9. monarchy _____

_____

10. Magna Carta _____

_____

Write!

Write your response to the prompt on a separate sheet of paper.
Use as many vocabulary words as you can in your writing.

Choose one of the documents you read about. How, do you think, did that document serve as a foundation for the United States constitution?

confederation   compromise   reserved powers   checks and balances

convention   democracy   separation of powers   amendment

delegates   federalism

How would you create a new form of government, one that no other country had? Read this selection to find out how the United States government was created.

The Constitution

The Articles of Confederation

In 1781, the original 13 states set up a national government. The Articles of Confederation laid out the new nation's government. A **confederation** is a group of independent states that work together. The first national government was weak. It had no leader or president. There were no courts to rule over all the states. The new government was not working. Changes had to be made.

The Constitutional Convention

In May 1787, the Constitutional Convention met in Philadelphia. A **convention** is a meeting for a particular purpose. **Delegates**, people chosen to speak and vote for a group, from 12 states were there. The delegates did not always agree.

George Washington was the leader of the Constitutional Convention.

States with many people thought they should have more power. States with fewer people wanted equal power. A compromise was made. In a **compromise**, each side gives up something to reach an agreement.

The Great Compromise

Plan A	Plan B
• Congress has two houses. • The number of representatives is based on population.	• Congress has one house. • Each state has the same number of representatives.

- Congress has two houses.
- In one house, the number of representatives is based on state population.
- In the other house, each state has the same number of representatives.

The Constitution

In 1788, the United States Constitution was approved. The Constitution created a **democracy**, a system of government run by the people who live under it. It also set up a system known as federalism. Under **federalism**, state and national governments share power and duties. Powers given to the states are called **reserved powers**. States, for example, have the right to create public schools. Each state also has the right to control business within its borders.

The Constitution created three branches of government. They are the legislative, executive and judicial branches. The separation of the government into three branches is called the **separation of powers**. It keeps one branch of government from becoming more powerful than others.

The writers of the constitution also included checks and balances. **Checks and balances** is a system in which each branch of government can limit the actions of the other branches. For example, the president can check the power of the Congress. He can block a law Congress passed by voting "no."

The Bill of Rights

After the Constitution was approved, it became clear that it had a flaw. It did not protect people's basic rights. Ten amendments were added to the Constitution. Each **amendment**, or change, protects our rights. The first ten amendments to the Constitution are known as the Bill of Rights.

My Social Studies Vocabulary

Go to page 94 to list other words you have learned about the Constitution.

confederation   compromise   reserved powers   checks and balances

convention   democracy   separation of powers   amendment

delegates   federalism

A. Fill in the blanks with the correct vocabulary word.

1. a change to a document

    — — — — — — — — —

2. a system of government in which powers and duties are shared
    between states and national governments

    — — — — — — — — — —

3. a group of independent states working together

    — — — — — — — — — — — — —

4. an agreement in which each side gets part of what it wants

    — — — — — — — — — —

5. powers given to the states

    — — — — — — — —   — — — — — —

6. a meeting that has a particular purpose

    — — — — — — — — — —

7. a system in which each branch of government can limit
    the actions of the other branches

    — — — — — —   — — —   — — — — — — — —

8. the separation of the government into three branches

    — — — — — — — — — —
    — — — — — — — —

9. people chosen to speak and vote for a group

    — — — — — — — — —

10. a form of government that gets its power from the people

    — — — — — — — — —

confederation	compromise	reserved powers	checks and balances
convention	democracy	separation of powers	amendment
delegates	federalism		

B. *Choose and write the two words that best complete each sentence.*

checks and balances	amendment	reserved powers	delegates

1. In May of 1787, the _____ created a system of

   _____ so no branch of government would be too powerful.

federalism	checks and balances	delegates	democracy

2. The Constitution created a _____ , a government run by

   the people, as well as a system of _____ , in which state

   and national governments share power.

compromise	reserved powers	convention	confederation

3. A _____ unites people at a meeting place, but

   a _____ is a group of states working together.

reserved powers	convention	separation of powers	federalism

4. Do not confuse the _____ , the three branches of

   government, with _____ , the powers given to the states.

amendment	checks and balances	democracy	compromise

5. The writers were able to reach a _____ , and all agreed to

   add an _____ protecting freedom of speech.

WORD ROOT

The word **democracy** comes from the Greek word **demokratia**, which means "rule of the people."

confederation   compromise   reserved powers   checks and balances

convention   democracy   separation of powers   amendment

delegates   federalism

C. *Choose the correct vocabulary word to complete each sentence.*

1. Under the system of _____ , the president can limit the power of Congress.

2. A state's _____ include the right to create public schools.

3. Powers and duties are shared between states and the national government under the system of _____ .

4. Everybody gets part of what they want in a _____ .

5. Most people thought that their _____ represented them well.

6. Three branches of government create a _____ .

7. When the Constitution needs to be changed, an _____ is added.

8. The first government of the United States was a _____ of states.

9. In a _____ , everyone has a voice in how the government is run.

10. Men from 12 states met at a _____ to create a new plan for governing the United States.

confederation	compromise	reserved powers	checks and balances
convention	democracy	separation of powers	amendment
delegates	federalism		

D. *Use each word in a sentence that shows you understand the meaning of the word.*

1. amendment _____

   _____

2. compromise _____

   _____

3. confederation _____

   _____

4. separation of powers _____

   _____

5. convention _____

   _____

6. reserved powers _____

   _____

7. democracy _____

   _____

8. federalism _____

   _____

9. checks and balances _____

   _____

10. delegates _____

    _____

Write! _____

Write your response to the prompt on a separate sheet of paper.
Use as many vocabulary words as you can in your writing.

What were some potential problems faced by the writers of the Constitution?
How did they solve them?

What would be the hardest thing about being the first president of the United States? Read this selection to find out about George Washington's challenges.

The Early Years of the United States

Building the New Government

The Constitution did not say much about how the **executive branch** should be run. This part of the government carries out the laws. The president is the head of the executive branch. The group of people who give him advice makes up his **cabinet**. During George Washington's **administration**, or time in office, many decisions were made that set the country on the right path.

President George Washington sits with members of his cabinet.

Building a Strong Country

Cabinet members are heads of departments. The **treasury** is the department in charge of collecting taxes and managing public funds. Alexander Hamilton was the first secretary of the treasury. The head of a department is called a secretary.

Washington's Cabinet	
Secretary	**Department**
Henry Knox	Department of War
Alexander Hamilton	Department of the Treasury
Thomas Jefferson	Department of State
Edmund Randolph	Attorney General

Hamilton wanted to set up a national bank. It would hold the taxes collected by the government.

Thomas Jefferson did not agree. He said that a national bank would give the national government too much power.

The controversy between Jefferson and Hamilton divided the new government. **Controversy** is a public disagreement between two sides with opposite views. However, Hamilton won out. In 1791, the Bank of the United States was created.

Hamilton suggested new sources of revenue. **Revenue** is the income that a government collects to pay for public expenses. Hamilton wanted to place a **tariff**, or tax, on all goods brought into the country. The duty would make the imports cost more. More people might then buy cheaper goods made in the United States.

Thomas Jefferson   Alexander Hamilton

Does the government have too much power? This controversy begun by Jefferson and Hamilton has continued to the present day.

During the Whiskey Rebellion, farmers poured tar over officers collecting taxes. They then covered them with feathers.

An excise tax on whiskey came next. An **excise tax** is money paid by the maker or seller of a product. Farmers from western Pennsylvania rebelled. They made whiskey from their extra corn. They then traded the whiskey for the things they needed. They did not have cash to pay the tax. Washington sent soldiers to put an end to the fight. This showed that the national government had the power to make people obey the law.

Building Foreign Policy

In 1789, the French Revolution broke out. The French were fighting for the same rights that the Americans had just won. The French expected help. But Washington declared **neutrality**. This is a policy of not taking sides in a war. A **policy** is a plan of action. Washington wanted to build a strong, successful nation. He hoped that avoiding war would allow that to happen.

My Social Studies Vocabulary

Go to page 95 to list other words you have learned about the early years of the United States.

| executive branch | administration | controversy | tariff | neutrality |
| cabinet | treasury | revenue | excise tax | policy |

A. *Fill in the blanks with the correct vocabulary word.*

1. money paid by the maker or seller of a product

   — — — — — —   — — —

2. the time during which a United States president holds office

   — — — — — — — — — — — — — —

3. a plan of action

   — — — — — —

4. a public disagreement between two sides with opposite views

   — — — — — — — — — — —

5. the part of the government that carries out the laws

   — — — — — — — — —   — — — — — —

6. a policy of not taking sides in a war

   — — — — — — — — — —

7. the group of people who give advice to the president

   — — — — — — —

8. the income that a government collects to pay for public expenses

   — — — — — — —

9. the department in charge of collecting taxes and managing public funds

   — — — — — — — —

10. a tax on goods brought into a country

    — — — — — —

| executive branch | administration | controversy | tariff | neutrality |
| cabinet | treasury | revenue | excise tax | policy |

B. *Choose and write the two words that best complete each sentence.*

| tariff | neutrality | policy | revenue |

1. One way the government collects _____ is to place
   a _____ on goods brought into the country.

| administration | treasury | tariff | excise tax |

2. During Washington's _____ , farmers in western Pennsylvania
   rebelled against the _____ on whiskey.

| cabinet | controversy | treasury | policy |

3. The first secretary of the _____ stirred up
   _____ by trying to set up a national bank.

| controversy | executive branch | policy | neutrality |

4. When the French Revolution broke out, Washington declared that
   _____ would be the _____ of
   the United States.

| treasury | cabinet | executive branch | excise tax |

5. The _____ is made up of the president and
   his _____ .

WORD ROOT

The word **neutrality** comes from the Latin
word **neutralis**, which means "middle ground."

| executive branch | administration | controversy | tariff | neutrality |
| cabinet | treasury | revenue | excise tax | policy |

C. *Choose the correct vocabulary word to complete each sentence.*

1. Hamilton's bank plan caused _____ because some people felt it would give too much power to the government.

2. The president is the head of the _____ of government.

3. The maker of a product might need to pay an _____ on it.

4. Washington hoped that _____ would allow the United States to stay strong.

5. The government department that collects and manages money is the _____ .

6. Taxes are one source of government _____ .

7. As secretary of the treasury, Alexander Hamilton was a member of Washington's _____ .

8. A president's _____ lasts as long as his term in office.

9. By placing a _____ on imports, Hamilton hoped people would buy cheaper American goods.

10. Washington's _____ of neutrality meant that the United States would not take sides in the French Revolution.

The Early Years of the United States

| executive branch | administration | controversy | tariff | neutrality |
| cabinet | treasury | revenue | excise tax | policy |

D. *Use each word in a sentence that shows you understand the meaning of the word.*

1. excise tax _____

_____

2. neutrality _____

_____

3. administration _____

_____

4. controversy _____

_____

5. policy _____

_____

6. executive branch _____

_____

7. revenue _____

_____

8. cabinet _____

_____

9. tariff _____

_____

10. treasury _____

_____

Write!

Write your response to the prompt on a separate sheet of paper. Use as many vocabulary words as you can in your writing.

Even though George Washington had no examples on which to base his presidency, he was still a strong leader. What made George Washington a strong president?

The presidents who followed Washington worked on building the nation. But they could not avoid dealing with the rest of the world. Read this selection to find out why.

The New Nation and the World

British Threats to American Shipping

Great Britain was opposed to the French Revolution and became France's enemy. Great Britain tried to **blockade** France. But the British could only partly prevent ships from entering or leaving French ports. Then the British began to seize American ships. The British needed more sailors. They claimed that American sailors were British and impressed them into the British navy. To **impress** is to force a person into military service.

American sailors were impressed because the British needed people to work on their ships.

But the thousands of impressed sailors were not British.

In 1807, President Thomas Jefferson tried to solve the problem. He ordered an **embargo**, or ban, on goods leaving America. That kept American ships at home. Jefferson hoped this action would force Great Britain and France to honor American neutrality. Instead, it hurt American trade.

The War of 1812

In 1812, President James Madison decided to go to war. He thought that the United States could gain Canada in the war against Great Britain. But the British won most of the early battles. They even captured Washington, D.C.

At last, Great Britain and the United States declared an **armistice**. It put an end to the fighting. Neither country gained any territory. **Territory** is land under the control of a country. But the United States showed that it could stand up to the world's strongest power. The war led to a rise of **nationalism**, meaning that Americans had more pride in their country.

When James Monroe became president, he worked on keeping the nation strong. In 1823, he presented a doctrine. A **doctrine** is a statement of government policy. The Monroe Doctrine warned Europe not to set up new colonies in the Americas. It promised that the United States would stay out of Europe's affairs.

The Monroe Doctrine set policy for the Americas.

The Age of Jackson

Andrew Jackson won the 1828 election by a **landslide**. He received a large majority of votes. After Jackson took office, he fired many government workers. He gave their jobs to people who helped him get elected. The practice of giving jobs to supporters is called the **spoils system**.

President Jackson did not approve of the Bank of the United States. He thought it had too much power over state banks. When it came time to renew the bank's contract, Jackson vetoed it. To **veto** means to say or vote "no."

Andrew Jackson was a general and a hero of the War of 1812.

> ### My Social Studies Vocabulary
> Go to page 95 to list other words you have learned about the new nation and the world.

blockade	embargo	territory	doctrine	spoils system
impress	armistice	nationalism	landslide	veto

A. *Match each word with its meaning. Write the letter of the correct meaning on the line in front of each word.*

1. _____ territory

2. _____ spoils system

3. _____ nationalism

4. _____ doctrine

5. _____ impress

6. _____ veto

7. _____ embargo

8. _____ landslide

9. _____ blockade

10. _____ armistice

a. the winning of an election by a very large majority of votes

b. to say or vote "no"

c. to force a person into military service

d. a statement of government policy

e. to prevent ships from entering or leaving a port

f. an end to fighting

g. the practice of giving jobs to supporters

h. land under the control of a country

i. pride in one's country

j. a ban on exporting goods

The New Nation and the World

blockade	embargo	territory	doctrine	spoils system
impress	armistice	nationalism	landslide	veto

B. *Circle the word that makes sense in each sentence. Then write the word.*

1. Andrew Jackson won the 1828 election by a (blockade, landslide).

   _____

2. The British would (veto, impress) American sailors into the British navy.

   _____

3. The United States hoped to gain (armistice, territory) in Canada.

   _____

4. The War of 1812 led to a rise in (nationalism, doctrine) among the

   American people. _____

5. Some people thought the (spoils system, doctrine) was bad because it gave jobs

   to people who were not qualified. _____

6. Tired of war, the two countries called for an (embargo, armistice).

   _____

7. When a country tries to (blockade, veto) a port, ships cannot enter or leave.

   _____

8. President Jefferson's (veto, embargo) on exports hurt American trade.

   _____

9. President Jackson decided to (blockade, veto) the new contract for the

   Bank of the United States. _____

10. President Monroe's (doctrine, landslide) put an end to new colonies being

    created in the Americas. _____

 **ROOT**

The word **nationalism** has its roots in the
Latin word **nasci**, meaning "to be born."

blockade	embargo	territory	doctrine	spoils system
impress	armistice	nationalism	landslide	veto

C. *Choose the correct vocabulary word to complete each sentence.*

1. The war ended when the nations called for an _____ .

2. The president has the right to _____ any law.

3. President Jefferson wanted an _____ to force Great Britain and France to accept the neutrality of the United States.

4. On the Fourth of July, people show their _____ by waving flags.

5. Because the British needed sailors, they might _____ an American sailor into the British navy.

6. Jackson was the first president to use the _____ to fill government jobs.

7. After the War of 1812, Great Britain kept its _____ in Canada.

8. Great Britain's attempt to _____ French ports was only partly successful.

9. President Monroe set forth a _____ to prevent European countries from gaining more control in the Americas.

10. Someone who wins an election by a _____ wins a very large majority of the votes.

The New Nation and the World

blockade	embargo	territory	doctrine	spoils system
impress	armistice	nationalism	landslide	veto

D. *Use each pair of words in a sentence.*

1. blockade, territory

   _____

   _____

   _____

2. embargo, impress

   _____

   _____

   _____

3. doctrine, nationalism

   _____

   _____

   _____

4. landslide, spoils system

   _____

   _____

   _____

5. veto, armistice

   _____

   _____

   _____

Write!

Write your response to the prompt on a separate sheet of paper. Use as many vocabulary words as you can in your writing.

Explain the steps that the United States took to deal with other countries during the early 1800s.

| opportunity | adjoining | turnpike | canal | ordinance |
| pioneer | frontier | technology | freight | homeland |

After the American Revolution, people began moving west of the Appalachian Mountains. Read this selection to find out how that movement enlarged the United States and brought more states into the union.

Settling the West

The Country Grows

People in the thirteen states were searching for cheaper land. They were also looking for better opportunities. An **opportunity** is a chance to make money or to better oneself. So, pioneers began moving to open land out West. A **pioneer** is one of the first people to settle an area.

Between 1800 and 1810, the population of Ohio increased from 45,000 to more than 230,000. The number of people in Kentucky, Tennessee, and the lands **adjoining**, or next to, them also grew.

The Louisiana Territory doubled the size of the United States.

In 1803, France sold the Louisiana Territory, which it had gained from Spain, to the United States. This new frontier doubled the size of the United States. A **frontier** is an area with few people at the edge of a settled region.

Settling the West

Improvements in Transportation

Travel to the West was not easy. Roads were rough, narrow trails. Soon private companies started building turnpikes. A **turnpike** is a road that travelers have to pay to use. Then the government built the National Road. It stretched from Maryland to Illinois.

Technology is the use of scientific knowledge to make machines and tools. It helped travel. The steamboat made river trips faster.

Robert Fulton's Clermont was the first successful steamboat. In 1807, it made its first trip up the Hudson River.

Not all bodies of water were connected. So, canals were dug. A **canal** is a waterway that connects two bodies of water. The Erie Canal was the first major canal in the United States. It greatly reduced the cost of moving people and freight. **Freight** is goods carried by a ship, truck, train, or airplane.

Settlers Go West

In 1787, Congress passed an **ordinance** so that lands north and west of the Ohio River could become states. This rule, or law, was called the Northwest Ordinance. It stated that a territory could apply to be a state once it had 60,000 people.

Native Americans fought back. They did not want white settlers on their land. In 1830, Congress passed the Indian Removal Act. Native Americans would be forced from their **homeland**, or land they came from. They would be resettled west of the Mississippi River.

So many Cherokee died on the trip from their homeland, they called it the "Trail of Tears."

> **My Social Studies Vocabulary**
>
> Go to page 95 to list other words you have learned about settling the West.

| opportunity | adjoining | turnpike | canal | ordinance |
| pioneer | frontier | technology | freight | homeland |

A. *Fill in the blanks with the correct vocabulary word.*

1. the use of scientific knowledge to make machines and tools

   — — — — — — — — — —

2. the goods carried by a truck, train, ship, or airplane

   — — — — — — —

3. a chance to make money or to better oneself

   — — — — — — — — — — —

4. one of the first people to settle an area

   — — — — — — —

5. next to

   — — — — — — — — —

6. a road that travelers have to pay to use

   — — — — — — — —

7. the land that a person comes from

   — — — — — — — —

8. a rule or law passed by a government

   — — — — — — — — —

9. a waterway dug across land to connect two bodies of water

   — — — — —

10. an area with few people at the edge of a settled region

    — — — — — — — —

Settling the West

| opportunity | adjoining | turnpike | canal | ordinance |
| pioneer | frontier | technology | freight | homeland |

B. *Choose and write the two words that best complete each sentence.*

| turnpike | opportunity | canal | frontier |

1. A pioneer might move to the _____ for cheap land and a new _____ .

| adjoining | homeland | ordinance | freight |

2. Kentucky, Tennessee, and _____ territories became states under the _____ passed in 1787.

| canal | turnpike | technology | pioneer |

3. The building of a _____ made it much easier for a _____ to travel by ship.

| frontier | freight | homeland | technology |

4. The development of new _____ made it easier for settlers to move into Native Americans' _____ .

| opportunity | turnpike | freight | ordinance |

5. It cost more to ship _____ on a _____ than on a public highway.

WORD ROOT

The word **opportunity** is based on the Latin word **opportunus**, meaning "favorable."

| opportunity | adjoining | turnpike | canal | ordinance |
| pioneer | frontier | technology | freight | homeland |

C. *Choose the correct vocabulary word to complete each sentence.*

1. Native Americans did not want to move away from their

    _____ .

2. Technology made it possible to travel by steamboat on a

    _____ that connected two rivers.

3. The cost of carrying _____ , such as farm goods,

    was much higher by land than by canal.

4. Pioneers paid a fee to go on a _____ , but the road

    was much easier to travel.

5. Once the United States purchased the Louisiana Territory, many pioneers

    moved to the new _____ .

6. People moved west because it was an _____ to get land.

7. The steamboat is an example of _____ that made travel

    faster and easier.

8. People moved to states _____ unsettled land.

9. Congress passed an _____ in 1787 so that territories

    north and west of the Ohio River could become states.

10. Until turnpikes and the first highway were built, a _____

    had to travel on rough, narrow trails.

D. *Use each word in a sentence that shows you understand the meaning of the word.*

1. frontier _____

    _____

2. turnpike _____

    _____

3. ordinance _____

    _____

4. opportunity _____

    _____

5. freight _____

    _____

6. canal _____

    _____

7. homeland _____

    _____

8. technology _____

    _____

9. pioneer _____

    _____

10. adjoining _____

    _____

Write! _____

Write your response to the prompt on a separate sheet of paper.
Use as many vocabulary words as you can in your writing.

Imagine that you own a company that wants to build a road or a canal. Write
a letter to the government explaining why the road or canal should be built.

Americans believed it was their mission to extend the borders of the United States "from sea to shining sea." How do you think the nation was able to expand from coast to coast? Read this selection to find out.

An Expanding Nation

Adding Territory

During the 1840s, Americans believed that the United States had the right to spread its rule. It was clear to them that the country should extend its boundaries from the Atlantic Ocean to the Pacific Ocean. A **boundary** is a border. A newspaper writer made up a phrase for this new belief. He called it **Manifest Destiny**.

Oregon Country

The nation's **expansion**, or increase in size, involved taking land claimed by other countries. Oregon Country was a huge area in the Northwest. The United States and Great Britain had jointly owned the land. In 1846, they agreed to divide it. The dividing line was 49 degrees north latitude. **Latitude** is the distance north or south of the equator. The equator is an imaginary line around the middle of Earth. Great Britain got the land above 49 degrees north latitude. The United States got the land below it. That land later became Oregon, Washington, and Idaho.

Oregon Country, 1846

In 1846, the Oregon Country was split between the United States and Great Britain at 49°N latitude.

Texas

Texas was once part of Mexico. Mexico itself was part of Spain. In 1821, Mexico broke free from Spain. It then offered Americans land grants to settle in Texas. A **land grant** is public land given by a government. The Texas settlers grew unhappy with the Mexican government. In 1836, they fought for independence and won. Texas asked to be annexed to the United States. To **annex** means to add to something larger or more important. In 1845, Texas became a state.

California and Other Western Territories

California and New Mexico were once part of Mexico, too. The United States wanted to buy those lands, but Mexico refused to sell. The United States went to war and defeated Mexico. In 1848, Mexico had to give much of its territory to the United States. This land now forms the states of California, Arizona, Nevada, and Utah. It also makes up parts of New Mexico, Colorado, and Wyoming.

After the Mexican-American War, California was admitted as a state.

Adding Markets

The need for new markets was one reason that expansion was important. Goods could be sold more cheaply due to **mass production**. This is the process of making things in large amounts, usually by machine. An **economy** is all the business dealings of a country or state. In the United States, the economy is based on **capitalism**. In this system, privately owned businesses control the production of goods. Under capitalism, entrepreneurs are always looking for new markets. An **entrepreneur** is someone who starts a business. That person takes all the risks but gets all the profits.

> **My Social Studies Vocabulary**
>
> Go to page 96 to list other words you have learned about the expanding nation.

boundary expansion land grant mass production capitalism

Manifest Destiny latitude annex economy entrepreneur

A. *Match each word with its meaning. Write the letter of the correct meaning on the line in front of each word.*

1. _____ land grant

2. _____ entrepreneur

3. _____ boundary

4. _____ annex

5. _____ economy

6. _____ capitalism

7. _____ Manifest Destiny

8. _____ expansion

9. _____ mass production

10. _____ latitude

a. to add to something larger or more important

b. a border

c. a person who starts a business, taking all the risks but getting all the profits

d. the process of making large quantities of things by machine

e. an increase in size

f. all the business dealings of a country or state

g. the distance north or south of the equator

h. public land given by a government

i. a system in which privately owned businesses control production

j. the belief that the United States had the right to extend its boundaries from the Atlantic Ocean to the Pacific Ocean

An Expanding Nation

boundary	expansion	land grant	mass production	capitalism
Manifest Destiny	latitude	annex	economy	entrepreneur

B. *Circle the word that makes sense in each sentence. Then write the word.*

1. Mexico gave a (mass production, land grant) to any American who wanted to live in Texas. _____

2. During the 1840s, Americans were interested in (expansion, latitude) to the West Coast. _____

3. People who believed in (economy, Manifest Destiny) thought that the United States should expand westward. _____

4. It can be risky for an (entrepreneur, annex) to start a business, but it can also be profitable. _____

5. The United States economy operates under a system called (boundary, capitalism). _____

6. Using lines of (latitude, annex) was an easy way to divide territory because many places in the West did not have names. _____

7. Americans wanted the Western (latitude, boundary) of the United States to extend to the Pacific Ocean. _____

8. People no longer had to make each item by hand once (mass production, capitalism) was introduced. _____

9. Private business, not the government, controls production in the United States (economy, entrepreneur). _____

10. The United States decided to (annex, land grant) Texas. _____

WORD ROOT

The word **expansion** comes from the Latin word **expandere**, meaning "to spread out."

| boundary | expansion | land grant | mass production | capitalism |
| Manifest Destiny | latitude | annex | economy | entrepreneur |

C. *Choose the correct vocabulary word to complete each sentence.*

1. The United States decided to _____ Texas, which became a state in 1845.

2. More goods were produced through _____ .

3. The United States has an _____ in which private businesses control how goods are made.

4. In the United States, the growth of the economy depends on a system called _____ .

5. If someone is willing to take a risk and spend money on a new business, that person is an _____ .

6. The British kept the land in Oregon Country that was above 49 degrees north _____ .

7. The phrase used to describe the belief that the United States should extend its rule is _____ .

8. The need for new markets was one reason for the _____ of the nation.

9. In exchange for receiving a _____ from Mexico, an American agreed to become a Mexican citizen.

10. The Atlantic Ocean served as the _____ of the country on the East Coast.

boundary	expansion	land grant	mass production	capitalism
Manifest Destiny	latitude	annex	economy	entrepreneur

D. *Use each word in a sentence that shows you understand the meaning of the word.*

1. expansion _____

_____

2. latitude _____

_____

3. entrepreneur _____

_____

4. land grant _____

_____

5. annex _____

_____

6. Manifest Destiny _____

_____

7. capitalism _____

_____

8. boundary _____

_____

9. mass production _____

_____

10. economy _____

_____

Write!

Write your response to the prompt on a separate sheet of paper.
Use as many vocabulary words as you can in your writing.

Explain the factors that led the United States to expand during the 1840s.
Give examples of America's growth.

LESSON 8

boom   abolitionist   fugitive   conductor   radical

abolish   sectionalism   Underground Railroad   sue   secede

Changes in technology and transportation did little to change the South. Plantations still remained a way of life. Read this selection to learn how growing cotton indirectly divided the country and led to war.

The Road to War

The Issue of Slavery

Many farmers in South Carolina, Alabama, and Mississippi were cotton planters. They learned that soil planted with cotton year after year wore out. So many of them moved west into Texas. Production suddenly increased from six thousand bales of cotton a year to over two million bales. But the cotton **boom** had a down side. As cotton growing spread west, so did slavery.

A family works in a cotton field.

The Missouri Compromise

By the early 1800s, Northern states had abolished slavery. To **abolish** means to put an end to something. A person who worked to end slavery was called an **abolitionist**. The different views of slavery in the North and the South caused conflict. When Missouri asked to join the Union as a slave state, Northern states objected. Adding a slave state would give the South more power. The Missouri Compromise kept the balance of power. It let in Missouri as a slave state and added Maine as a free state. The plan also banned slavery in all territory north of Missouri.

In the South, feelings of **sectionalism** grew. Some people cared more about their section, or part, of the nation than the nation as a whole. Some Northerners called for an end to slavery in the South. Southerners whose living depended on slavery did not want to make the change. They accused Northerners of trying to destroy the South's economy.

The Underground Railroad

Slaves often ran away to the North. Southerners wanted Northerners to catch and return each **fugitive**, or runaway. Instead, abolitionists set up the **Underground Railroad**. It was a system of people who helped slaves escape. The tracks were not steel. They were back roads and rivers to the North. A **conductor** was a person who led a group to freedom. The conductors were often former slaves.

The Country Breaks Apart

In 1857, Dred Scott, a slave, sued for his freedom. To **sue** is to bring legal action to settle a disagreement. The Supreme Court ruled against him. They said that a slave was not a citizen. They also said that the Missouri Compromise was against the law. That meant that slavery could spread.

In 1860, Abraham Lincoln was elected president. He did not believe in slavery. Radicals in the South believed that the new president and Congress would turn against the South. A **radical** is a person who is in favor of extreme changes. By 1861, eleven Southern states voted to **secede**. They left the United States to form a new nation.

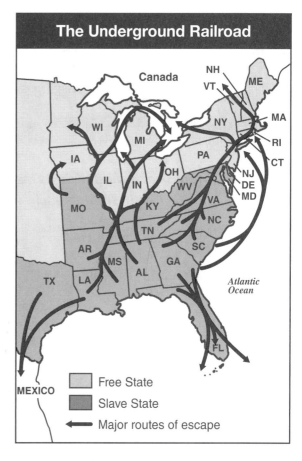

The Underground Railroad

Dred Scott sued for his freedom, but the Supreme Court ruled that slaves were not American citizens.

My Social Studies Vocabulary

Go to page 96 to list other words you have learned about the road to war.

boom   abolitionist   fugitive   conductor   radical

abolish   sectionalism   Underground Railroad   sue   secede

A. *Match each word with its meaning. Write the letter of the correct meaning on the line in front of each word.*

1. _____ conductor

2. _____ abolish

3. _____ radical

4. _____ boom

5. _____ secede

6. _____ sue

7. _____ sectionalism

8. _____ fugitive

9. _____ Underground Railroad

10. _____ abolitionist

a. to bring legal action to settle a disagreement

b. a sudden increase in production

c. a system of people who helped slaves escape

d. a person who worked to end slavery

e. a person who runs away

f. a person who is in favor of extreme changes

g. to put an end to something

h. to leave one country and form a new one

i. a person who led a group of slaves to freedom

j. loyalty to one's region rather than to the country as a whole

boom	abolitionist	fugitive		conductor	radical
abolish	sectionalism	Underground Railroad		sue	secede

B. *Circle the word that makes sense in each sentence. Then write the word.*

1. A Southern (fugitive, radical) was someone who thought the South should secede. _____

2. Feelings of (sectionalism, abolitionist) were beginning to push the North and South apart. _____

3. Slaves escaped to freedom in the North by using the (Underground Railroad, radical). _____

4. Growing cotton in Texas resulted in a (conductor, boom) in production. _____

5. Eleven Southern states voted to (secede, abolish) from the United States by 1861. _____

6. On the Underground Railroad, a (radical, conductor) led slaves out of the South to safety. _____

7. A Northerner who thought slavery was wrong might become an (Underground Railroad, abolitionist). _____

8. People in the South were angry that Northerners refused to return any slave who was a (fugitive, radical). _____

9. The Northern states' desire to (abolish, secede) slavery caused conflict with the Southern states. _____

10. Dred Scott tried to (sue, secede) to gain his freedom. _____

WORD ROOT

Secede comes from the Latin word **secedere**, meaning "to go apart."

| boom | abolitionist | fugitive | | conductor | radical |
| abolish | sectionalism | Underground Railroad | sue | secede |

C. *Choose the correct vocabulary word to complete each sentence.*

1. The Supreme Court said that a slave was not a citizen and could not

   _____ for his freedom.

2. More than one _____ was responsible for getting

   the South to secede from the United States.

3. Over two million bales of cotton were produced each year during the

   cotton _____ .

4. Southerners decided to _____ after Lincoln became

   president because they did not believe he shared their interest in keeping slavery.

5. When Northerners rescued fugitive slaves rather than catching and returning

   them, feelings of _____ increased in the South.

6. The Southern states did not agree with the Northern states' decision

   to _____ slavery.

7. Back roads and rivers made up the "tracks" of the _____ .

8. Sometimes, a slave who escaped came back to the South to be

   a _____ on the Underground Railroad.

9. Ending slavery was the goal of an _____ .

10. The purpose of the Underground Railroad was to help a _____

    slave escape from the Southern slave states.

The Road to War

| boom | abolitionist | fugitive | | conductor | radical |
| abolish | sectionalism | Underground Railroad | sue | secede |

D. *Use each word in a sentence that shows you understand the meaning of the word.*

1. abolitionist _____

    _____

2. secede _____

    _____

3. sue _____

    _____

4. Underground Railroad _____

    _____

5. fugitive _____

    _____

6. radical _____

    _____

7. sectionalism _____

    _____

8. abolish _____

    _____

9. boom _____

    _____

10. conductor _____

    _____

Write! _____

Write your response to the prompt on a separate sheet of paper.
Use as many vocabulary words as you can in your writing.

Imagine that you live in the North or the South. Write a letter to a friend or family member, explaining your position on slavery.

civil war	Union	emancipation	riot	total war
Confederacy	defensive	draft	turning point	surrender

Was the Civil War worth its costs? Read this selection to find out what happened when Americans went to war against other Americans.

The Civil War

The War Begins

The Civil War split the United States into North and South. A **civil war** is a war between groups in the same country. The group of Southern states that left the nation was called the **Confederacy**. The **Union** was the group of Northern states that remained.

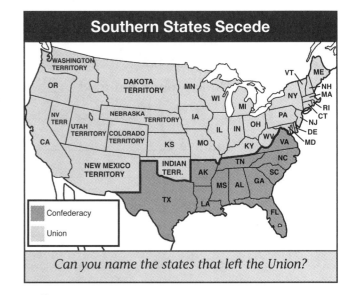

Southern States Secede

Confederacy
Union

Can you name the states that left the Union?

Northerners did not think the Civil War would last long. The Union had more people to serve in the army. It had more factories to build weapons and more railroads to transport soldiers. Its ships could block Southern ports to stop trade with Europe.

The Confederacy, however, had strong military leaders, such as General Robert E. Lee. And its soldiers were well trained. Also, the South was mostly fighting a **defensive** war on its own land. It did everything it could to protect against attack.

The Civil War

The Emancipation of the Slaves

The North had gone to war to unite the country. Its goal was not to end slavery. But in 1863, President Lincoln freed all slaves in the Southern states that had left the Union. Lincoln hoped that the **emancipation**, or freeing, of the slaves would weaken the South and help end the war.

President Lincoln says slaves in Confederate states are free.

War Takes Its Toll

When the war began in 1861, soldiers on both sides signed up eagerly. Soon, however, people lost hope. Both sides had to draft soldiers. To **draft** means to choose someone from a group to serve in the armed forces. In the North, riots broke out. A **riot** is a crowd of people who become out of control.

African Americans did not need to be drafted into the Union army — they wanted to serve.

The Confederacy won many battles in the early years of the war. The Battle of Gettysburg, in 1863, marked a **turning point**, or major change. The Confederate army attacked but lost. Never again would it have the strength to invade the North.

The Battle of Gettysburg was a turning point in the Civil War.

Victory for the North

In the end, the North won the Civil War. One reason was its practice of **total war**. The North attacked civilians and resources as well as the army. Anything useful to the enemy, such as food, buildings, and equipment, was destroyed. In April 1865, the Southern army surrendered. To **surrender** means to declare that an enemy has won and that fighting can stop. The Civil War ended with more than 600,000 dead.

My Social Studies Vocabulary

Go to page 96 to list other words you have learned about the Civil War.

civil war	Union	emancipation	riot	total war
Confederacy	defensive	draft	turning point	surrender

A. *Fill in the blanks with the correct vocabulary word.*

1. to choose someone from a group to serve in the armed forces

    — — — — —

2. done to protect against attack

    — — — — — — — — —

3. to declare that the enemy has won and that fighting can stop

    — — — — — — — — —

4. a war between groups in the same country

    — — — — — — — —

5. a crowd of people who become out of control

    — — — —

6. the act of setting people free

    — — — — — — — — — — — —

7. the Northern states that remained in the nation

    — — — — —

8. an event that changes the way things are going

    — — — — — — — — — — — —

9. the group of Southern states that left the nation

    — — — — — — — — — — —

10. a war against civilians and resources as well as against an army

    — — — — — — — —

civil war	Union	emancipation	riot	total war
Confederacy	defensive	draft	turning point	surrender

B. *Choose and write the two words that best complete each sentence.*

Confederacy	total war	civil war	turning point

1. When an important battle is a _____ in a
   _____ , one side may seem to be set to win.

emancipation	Confederacy	draft	Union

2. During the Civil War, the _____ in the South fought against
   the _____ in the North.

defensive	draft	surrender	total war

3. The South fought a _____ war on its own land but suffered
   the effects of _____ on its people and resources.

surrender	riot	draft	emancipation

4. When the North was forced to _____ people into the army,
   a _____ broke out.

emancipation	draft	surrender	riot

5. The South did not _____ to the North until two years after
   Lincoln declared the _____ of the slaves.

WORD ROOT

The word **Union** comes from the Latin word **unus**, meaning "one."

The Civil War

civil war	Union	emancipation	riot	total war
Confederacy	defensive	draft	turning point	surrender

C. *Choose the correct vocabulary word to complete each sentence.*

1. President Lincoln hoped that the _____ of the slaves would weaken the South.

2. Angry Northerners started a _____ when they learned that they might be drafted into the armed forces.

3. The practice of _____ against the South was successful because it affected all its people and resources, not just its army.

4. The Southern states of the _____ seceded from the nation to defend their way of life.

5. When two groups within the same country strongly disagree about something, the result could be a _____ .

6. When there are not enough soldiers to fight a war, a government might have to _____ people.

7. The South was forced to fight a _____ war to protect its land and people.

8. The original goal of the _____ was to unite the country again.

9. Winning the Battle of Gettysburg was a _____ for the North, which had lost many earlier battles.

10. The Civil War ended when the Southern army decided to _____ .

civil war   Union   emancipation   riot   total war
Confederacy   defensive   draft   turning point   surrender

D. *Use each word in a sentence that shows you understand the meaning of the word.*

1. emancipation _____

_____

2. surrender _____

_____

3. civil war _____

_____

4. riot _____

_____

5. Confederacy _____

_____

6. total war _____

_____

7. Union _____

_____

8. defensive _____

_____

9. turning point _____

_____

10. draft _____

_____

Write! _____

Write your response to the prompt on a separate sheet of paper.
Use as many vocabulary words as you can in your writing.

Suppose the Civil War has just ended. How would people living in the North
and those living in the South differ in their views of the war?

assassination   freedmen   tenant farmer   inherit   carpetbagger
Reconstruction sharecropper   black codes   segregation scalawag

During Reconstruction, the government worked to rebuild the South and to bring it back into the Union. How do you think Southerners felt about the changes that were happening? Read this selection to find out.

Reconstruction

Reconstruction and President Lincoln

The Thirteenth Amendment ended slavery in 1865. But President Lincoln never got a chance to see the change. The law passed just after his assassination. An **assassination** is the killing of a public figure. Lincoln had hoped to rebuild the South and bring it back into the United States. This plan was called **Reconstruction**. It happened without him.

The State of the South

The South lay in ruins. Cities and railroads were destroyed. A way of life was gone. Nearly forty million **freedmen**, former slaves, had no jobs or education. Many became sharecroppers.

A **sharecropper** is a farmer who works someone else's land in return for a share of the crop. Sharecroppers made hardly enough to live on. Other freedmen became tenant farmers. A **tenant farmer** pays rent to work someone else's land.

A sharecropper worked very hard but stayed poor.

Southern Actions

Southern states wanted to limit the rights that freedmen had gained. So they passed laws called **black codes**. The laws said that freedmen could not vote, carry guns, or work skilled jobs. They could not own or inherit property. **Inherit** means to get something from someone after he or she has died.

Southern states also passed laws that separated people by race. This practice is called **segregation**. African Americans could not go to the same public places as whites.

Reconstruction Problems

In parts of the South, there was little law. A group calling itself the Ku Klux Klan formed. They claimed their goal was to bring law and order. But they worked against the goals of Reconstruction. They tried to strike fear into African Americans who dared to claim their rights.

Some Southerners viewed carpetbaggers as greedy robbers.

Many Northerners moved to the South during Reconstruction. Some went to help. Others went to make money. These people often carried their things in bags made of carpet. Southerners called such a person a **carpetbagger**. Some Southerners disliked carpetbaggers. They also disliked scalawags. A **scalawag** was a Southern white person who was in favor of Reconstruction.

In 1877, Reconstruction ended. The results were mixed. The North and the South were one country again. New amendments gave African Americans full rights, including the right to vote. Still, it would take almost a full century before African Americans would actually enjoy those rights.

My Social Studies Vocabulary

Go to page 97 to list other words you have learned about Reconstruction.

assassination   freedmen   tenant farmer   inherit   carpetbagger

Reconstruction   sharecropper   black codes   segregation   scalawag

A. *Match each word with its meaning. Write the letter of the correct meaning on the line in front of each word.*

1. _____ inherit

2. _____ freedmen

3. _____ sharecropper

4. _____ scalawag

5. _____ assassination

6. _____ tenant farmer

7. _____ Reconstruction

8. _____ segregation

9. _____ black codes

10. _____ carpetbagger

a. a farmer who works someone else's land in return for a share of the crops

b. laws that limited the rights of freedmen

c. the plan to rebuild the South and bring it back into the United States

d. the killing of a public figure

e. to get something from someone after he or she has died

f. a Southern name for a Northerner who moved to the South during Reconstruction

g. former slaves

h. the practice of separating people by race

i. a farmer who pays rent to work someone else's land

j. a Southern name for a Southern white person who was in favor of Reconstruction

| assassination | freedmen | tenant farmer | inherit | carpetbagger |
| Reconstruction | sharecropper | black codes | segregation | scalawag |

B. *Circle the word that makes sense in each sentence. Then write the word.*

1. Because a (tenant farmer, sharecropper) got paid in crops instead of money, he or she could never get ahead. _____

2. Abraham Lincoln's (assassination, black codes) did not stop plans for Reconstruction. _____

3. African Americans could not go to the same public places as whites under (Reconstruction, segregation). _____

4. Freedmen could not vote, carry guns, or work skilled jobs because of (segregation, black codes). _____

5. The name (carpetbagger, freedmen) came from the type of bag a Northerner carried. _____

6. A former slave might not have become a (sharecropper, tenant farmer) because it was difficult to save enough money for rent. _____

7. The rebuilding of the South after the Civil War is called (assassination, Reconstruction). _____

8. The men, women, and children who had been slaves before the Civil War were called (scalawags, freedmen). _____

9. Laws made it illegal for former slaves to own or (scalawag, inherit) property.

    _____

10. In the Southern states, a (tenant farmer, scalawag) was not liked.

    _____

WORD ROOT

The word **segregation** comes from the Latin word **segregare**, meaning "separate" or "isolate."

assassination   freedmen   tenant farmer   inherit   carpetbagger

Reconstruction   sharecropper   black codes   segregation   scalawag

C.   Choose the correct vocabulary word to complete each sentence.

1. President Lincoln's _____ occurred before Reconstruction.

2. It was difficult for African American families to get wealthy because they could not _____ property.

3. If someone from the South favored Reconstruction but was not a former slave, that person was called a _____ .

4. The Thirteenth Amendment freed African Americans, but laws known as _____ took away many of their rights.

5. If someone could afford to pay rent to farm land, that person became a _____ .

6. Without a job or education, _____ were not much better off than they had been as slaves.

7. An African-American farmer was more likely to be a _____ than a tenant farmer.

8. Some Southerners thought that a _____ from the North came only to make money.

9. The years between 1865 and 1877 were the time of _____ .

10. Black codes and _____ kept African Americans in the South from gaining their rights.

assassination   freedmen   tenant farmer   inherit   carpetbagger

Reconstruction   sharecropper   black codes   segregation   scalawag

D. *Use each word in a sentence that shows you understand the meaning of the word.*

1. assassination _____

   _____

2. inherit _____

   _____

3. black codes _____

   _____

4. freedmen _____

   _____

5. scalawag _____

   _____

6. tenant farmer _____

   _____

7. Reconstruction _____

   _____

8. carpetbagger _____

   _____

9. segregation _____

   _____

10. sharecropper _____

   _____

Write!

Write your response to the prompt on a separate sheet of paper.
Use as many vocabulary words as you can in your writing.

Do you think that Reconstruction was a success or a failure? Explain why you think so.

Machines play an important part in modern life. Could new machines change how you live? Could they change an entire country? Read this selection to learn how machines changed life in the United States after the Civil War.

Industrialization

During the 1800s, many people stopped farming for a living. Instead, they made goods in factories. A new age of industry began. Industry is the making of goods in a factory. The change to industry from farming is called **industrialization**.

Inventions

There were many new inventions during the 1800s. An **invention** is an original idea for making new things. Some inventions led to new products. Others improved how goods were made.

In the 1850s, a new process for making steel was developed. It helped lead to more railroads. In the West, thousands of workers were brought from China to help lay tracks. In 1869, a railroad joined the East and the West for the first time. It was a **transcontinental** railroad. It went across the whole continent.

The eastern tracks and the western tracks of the transcontinental railroad met in Utah.

Big Business Grows

In the early days of the nation, businesses were small. Often, they had just one owner. In the late 1800s, a new kind of business began. It was the corporation. A **corporation** is a business owned by many people. Each person owns a part, or share, of a business.

At first, there were few laws to **regulate**, or control, corporations. They could do what they wanted. For example, in the late 1800s, one oil company got bigger and bigger. It put other oil companies out of business. Finally, it became a **monopoly**. It controlled the whole industry.

This cartoon shows Standard Oil, a monopoly, crushing other businesses.

Labor Unions

Many people worked in sweatshops. A **sweatshop** is a small factory or mill with poor working conditions. People worked long hours—sometimes as many as 16 hours a day—for low pay. Children often worked in sweatshops, too.

Workers joined together to fight back. They formed labor unions. A **labor union** is a group of workers who join together to bring changes. Often, labor unions use a strike to get what they want. During a **strike**, people stop working to get higher pay or better conditions. Some strikes ended in bloodshed between workers and factory owners' "strike breakers."

What did these striking workers want?

Hard Times

Business did not always do well. In 1873 and 1893, panics occurred. During a **panic**, businesses fail. Jobs disappear, banks close, and families go hungry. People wondered why the government wasn't doing more to control business.

My Social Studies Vocabulary

Go to page 97 to list other words you have learned about industrialization.

Industrialization

industrialization   transcontinental   regulate   sweatshop   strike

invention   corporation   monopoly   labor union   panic

A. *Fill in the blanks with the correct vocabulary word.*

1. a time when businesses fail, people lose jobs, and banks close

    — — — — —

2. the change from farming to industry

    — — — — — — — — — — — — — — — — —

3. a stopping of work in order to get higher pay or better conditions

    — — — — — —

4. to control through laws

    — — — — — — — —

5. a company that controls an industry by getting rid of its competition

    — — — — — — — —

6. a small factory or mill with poor working conditions

    — — — — — — — — —

7. a group of workers who join together to bring changes

    — — — — —   — — — — —

8. a business owned by many people; each owns shares

    — — — — — — — — — — —

9. across the continent

    — — — — — — — — — — — — — — — —

10. an original idea for a new process or product

    — — — — — — — — —

industrialization   transcontinental   regulate   sweatshop   strike
invention   corporation   monopoly   labor union   panic

B. *Choose and write the two words that best complete each sentence.*

monopoly	panic	regulate	labor union

1. The government did not _____ the business, and it soon

   grew into a _____ .

corporation	sweatshop	invention	strike

2. The workers went on a _____ to try to change bad

   conditions in the _____ .

monopoly	industrialization	transcontinental	invention

3. The _____ of a new way to make steel helped lead to the

   _____ railroad.

strike	sweatshop	labor union	corporation

4. Members of a _____ tried to get better pay and better

   treatment from the _____ .

panic	regulate	transcontinental	industrialization

5. One problem that caused worry or suffering in the age of

   _____ was a _____ .

WORD ROOT

The word **corporation** comes from the Latin word **corporare**, which means "to make into a body."

Industrialization

67

industrialization   transcontinental   regulate   sweatshop   strike
invention   corporation   monopoly   labor union   panic

C. *Choose the correct vocabulary word to complete each sentence.*

1. The _____ railroad reached from the East to the West.

2. One company had a _____ on the whole oil business.

3. Because businesses failed, people lost their jobs during a
   _____ .

4. A new factory was built to produce the new _____ .

5. Many people own part of a business in a _____ .

6. Adults and children worked side by side in the dirty
   _____ .

7. The workers went on a _____ to try to shorten their
   workday.

8. People made many goods in factories during the age of
   _____ .

9. The corporation did what it wanted because the government did not
   _____ it.

10. The factory workers joined to form a _____ .

D. *Use each word in a sentence that shows you know the meaning of the word.*

1. strike _____

_____

2. panic _____

_____

3. labor union _____

_____

4. industrialization _____

_____

5. sweatshop _____

_____

6. transcontinental _____

_____

7. regulate _____

_____

8. invention _____

_____

9. corporation _____

_____

10. monopoly _____

_____

Write!

Write your response to the prompt on a separate sheet of paper.
Use as many vocabulary words as you can in your writing.

Describe some of the changes that occurred in the United States as a result of industrialization.

| urbanization | emigration | slum | ethnic group | suburb |
| immigrant | nativism | tenement | skyscraper | commute |

What causes cities to grow? What happens when cities grow fast? Read this selection to learn why cities grew and changed in the late 1800s.

The Growth of Cities

As industry grew, factories needed more workers. Many Americans moved from farms to fill factory jobs. As a result, cities grew. The growth of cities is called **urbanization**. But factories needed even more workers.

Immigrants

Immigrants came to America to fill factory jobs. An **immigrant** is a person who comes to live in a country.

In the 1800s, millions of immigrants came to the East. They came from Germany and Ireland. Later, immigrants from Italy, Russia, and Poland arrived.

Immigrants also came to the West. They came from China, Japan, and Mexico.

Poverty was one reason for **emigration**, leaving one's country to live in another. Millions of Irish left Ireland to avoid starving

Millions of immigrants came to the United States in the 1800s.

when crops failed. Others left to find freedom. Over a million Jews left Russia to find religious freedom in the United States.

Immigrants were not always welcomed. Some people who had been born in the United States saw them as "outsiders." They believed that "native-born" people should be favored over immigrants. Many believers in **nativism** wanted to stop immigration.

Life in the Cities

Cities could not change fast enough for all the people who were arriving. Housing was a big problem. As a result, slums developed. A **slum** is a poor, crowded part of a city. Many people in the slums lived in tenements. A **tenement** is a crowded apartment house.

In many cases, slums held people of the same ethnic group. An **ethnic group** is people with the same language, customs, culture, or country. For example, Russians chose to live with other Russians. Other groups did the same. They relied on one another for help.

In time, each new group of immigrants began to think of themselves as Americans. Eventually, ethnic groups got to know one another. They shared their customs and cultures.

Many immigrants lived in crowded tenements.

Other Changes in Cities

Cities did not just get bigger. They also got taller. At the end of the 1800s, people began to build a new kind of building. It was called the **skyscraper**. Skyscrapers grew taller and taller. They changed the look of cities.

Transportation in cities also changed. Electric streetcars, or trolleys, allowed people to live farther from their jobs. A person could live in a suburb and still work in the city. A **suburb** is an area just beyond the city limits. The streetcar made the **commute**, the trip to and from work, possible.

This early skyscraper was taller than everything around it.

My Social Studies Vocabulary

Go to page 97 to list other words you have learned about the growth of cities.

urbanization   emigration   slum   ethnic group   suburb
immigrant   nativism   tenement   skyscraper   commute

A. *Choose the word that best answers each question.*

1. I am a very tall building. What am I?

   slum   suburb   skyscraper

2. I am people with the same customs, language, culture, or country. What am I?

   ethnic group   immigrant   urbanization

3. I am a rundown, crowded apartment house. What am I?

   suburb   tenement   commute

4. I am the act of leaving one's home country. What am I?

   emigration   immigrant   tenement

5. I am a person who goes to another country to live. Who am I?

   emigration   ethnic group   immigrant

6. I am the belief that people born in a country should be favored over immigrants. What am I?

   skyscraper   slum   nativism

7. I am an area just beyond the city. What am I?

   nativism   ethnic group   suburb

8. I am the trip back and forth to work. What am I?

   commute   urbanization   immigrant

9. I am a crowded, poor part of a city. What am I?

   suburb   slum   emigration

10. I am the growth of cities. What am I?

    commute   skyscraper   urbanization

| urbanization | emigration | slum | ethnic group | suburb |
| immigrant | nativism | tenement | skyscraper | commute |

B. *Circle the word that makes sense in each sentence. Then write the word.*

1. Three families lived in the same apartment in the (urbanization, tenement).
   _____

2. The practice of favoring people born in a country over immigrants is (urbanization, nativism). _____

3. Irish people who lived with other Irish people wanted to be near their own (ethnic group, slum). _____

4. Cities grew more and more crowded as (commute, urbanization) occurred.
   _____

5. Some people who worked in the city traveled there from a (suburb, slum).
   _____

6. The look of cities was changed forever by the (ethnic group, skyscraper).
   _____

7. When an (emigration, immigrant) _____ arrived in the United States, he probably did not speak English.

8. People often got sick from dirty, crowded conditions in a (skyscraper, slum).
   _____

9. Bad conditions in a country were a reason for (emigration, immigrant).
   _____

10. The new streetcars helped people make their daily (commute, tenement) to work. _____

ROOT

The words **urbanization** and **suburb** come from the Latin root **urbs**, meaning "city."

The Growth of Cities

| urbanization | emigration | slum | ethnic group | suburb |
| immigrant | nativism | tenement | skyscraper | commute |

C. *Choose the correct vocabulary word to complete each sentence.*

1. The neighbors spoke the same language and belonged to the same _____ .

2. Just outside the city were the quiet streets of a _____ .

3. People took an elevator to the top floor of the _____ .

4. The family did not like their dirty rooms in the _____ .

5. There were many overcrowded buildings in the _____ .

6. Mr. Laska made his _____ to the city by streetcar.

7. The family said that lack of food was a reason for _____ from Ireland.

8. Hope for a better life was a reason for an _____ to come to the United States.

9. Immigrants were hurt by feelings of _____ .

10. Changes in transportation and buildings were part of _____ .

urbanization	emigration	slum	ethnic group	suburb
immigrant	nativism	tenement	skyscraper	commute

D. *Use each pair of words in a sentence.*

1. skyscraper, urbanization

   _____

   _____

2. immigrant, nativism

   _____

   _____

3. commute, suburb

   _____

   _____

4. emigration, ethnic group

   _____

   _____

5. slum, tenement

   _____

   _____

Write!

Write your response to the prompt on a separate sheet of paper.
Use as many vocabulary words as you can in your writing.

Imagine that you were an immigrant to the United States during the late 1800s. Tell about why you left your country, how you traveled, and what you experienced in the United States.

literacy test   Jim Crow laws   reformer   corruption   political machine

poll tax   suffrage   settlement house   kickback   muckraker

Some people didn't always have the right to vote in the United States. Read this selection to learn about this problem and others the United States faced in the late 1800s and early 1900s.

The Age of Reform

Problems for African Americans

In the late 1800s, states in the South passed many unfair laws. They tried to stop African Americans from voting. Some states said voters had to pass a literacy test. A **literacy test** checks a person's ability to read and write. Most slaves had not been taught to read or write. Now they were free, but they could not pass a literacy test.

States also started a poll tax. A **poll tax** is money that must be paid in order to vote. Many former slaves were too poor to pay the tax. They could not vote.

Amendments to the Constitution had given African Americans rights. But later court rulings took away or limited those rights. For example, in 1896, the Supreme Court ruled that "separate but equal" public places were legal. So, some states passed **Jim Crow laws**. These laws separated African Americans and whites in public places. Trains had separate cars for each race. The children of each race went to separate schools. There were even separate drinking fountains for the two races.

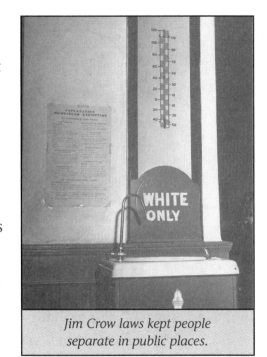

Jim Crow laws kept people separate in public places.

No Voting Rights for Women

Women also did not have equal rights. They could not vote in national elections. The right to vote is called **suffrage**. During the 1800s, women worked hard to be able to vote. Over time, they reached their goal. In 1920, women were able to vote in the national election.

These women voted in a national election for the first time in 1920.

Jane Addams

The fast growth of cities brought many problems. Jane Addams was a **reformer**, a person who works for change. She helped to change the poor conditions she saw in her city, Chicago. She founded Hull House. Hull House was a settlement house. A **settlement house** offers services to help poor people. Hull House offered classes. It had a playground and a music school.

Dishonest Government

Dishonest government also hurt cities. Many city officials made money through corruption. **Corruption** is lack of honesty. A corrupt city official might receive a kickback. A **kickback** is a payment to a person who controls a source of money.

At this time, political machines ran many cities. A **political machine** is an organized group of people in power. It trades favors for votes. It makes unfair deals to stay in power.

Some writers wrote about political machines. They wrote about other problems in the United States, too. A person who wrote about dishonest or unfair dealings was called a **muckraker**. The name comes from the dirty and often impossible job of raking up mud.

Upton Sinclair wrote about unhealthy conditions in the meat-packing industry.

My Social Studies Vocabulary

Go to page 98 to list other words you have learned about the age of reform.

The Age of Reform

literacy test   Jim Crow laws   reformer   corruption   political machine
poll tax   suffrage   settlement house kickback   muckraker

A. *Match each word with its meaning. Write the letter of the correct meaning on the line in front of each word.*

1. ____ corruption

2. ____ poll tax

3. ____ political machine

4. ____ kickback

5. ____ literacy test

6. ____ suffrage

7. ____ reformer

8. ____ settlement house

9. ____ muckraker

10. ____ Jim Crow laws

a. payment to a person who controls a source of money

b. the right to vote

c. laws passed by Southern states to keep the races separate

d. a person who works for change

e. a person who writes about secret illegal, unfair, or dishonest actions

f. a test of the ability to read and write

g. money that must be paid in order to be able to vote

h. lack of honesty

i. an organized group of people in government with power

j. a place that offers services to help poor people

The Age of Reform

literacy test	Jim Crow laws	reformer	corruption	political machine
poll tax	suffrage	settlement house	kickback	muckraker

B. *Choose and write the two words that best complete each sentence.*

Jim Crow laws	literacy test	poll tax	political machine

1. Two ways that states in the South tried to keep African Americans from voting were the _____ and the _____ .

political machine	reformer	muckraker	settlement house

2. The _____ wrote about the dishonest things that some members of the _____ did.

poll tax	settlement house	kickback	reformer

3. Jane Addams was a _____ who opened a _____ in Chicago.

corruption	suffrage	literacy test	kickback

4. A type of _____ occurred in city government when officials got a _____ .

suffrage	corruption	Jim Crow laws	muckraker

5. In the South, _____ kept African Americans and whites separate, while other laws denied women _____ , or the right to vote.

WORD ROOT

The word **literacy** comes from the Latin word **literae**, meaning "letters" or "literature."

literacy test   Jim Crow laws   reformer   corruption   political machine

poll tax   suffrage   settlement house   kickback   muckraker

C. *Choose the correct vocabulary word to complete each sentence.*

1. The city official received money as a _____ .

2. The poor people received help at the _____ .

3. A story about dishonesty in government was written by a

   _____ .

4. During the 1800s, African Americans and women did not have

   _____ .

5. Solving problems is the work of a _____ .

6. City governments were weakened by wrongdoing and other

   _____ .

7. In the South, African Americans attended separate schools because

   of _____ .

8. Many former slaves who could not read or write failed the

   _____ for voting.

9. Some people could not afford to pay the _____ ,
   so they could not vote.

10. Buying votes was one way that a _____ stayed in power.

The Age of Reform

literacy test   Jim Crow laws   reformer   corruption   political machine
poll tax   suffrage   settlement house   kickback   muckraker

D. *Use each word in a sentence that shows you understand the meaning of the word.*

1. poll tax _____

_____

2. reformer _____

_____

3. political machine _____

_____

4. Jim Crow laws _____

_____

5. settlement house _____

_____

6. muckraker _____

_____

7. literacy test _____

_____

8. corruption _____

_____

9. kickback _____

_____

10. suffrage _____

_____

Write!

Write your response to the prompt on a separate sheet of paper.
Use as many vocabulary words as you can in your writing.

You are a muckraker in the year 1900. Describe a topic you would like
to write an article about.

| imperialism | invest | cavalry | negotiate | foreign |
| revolt | guerrilla | protectorate | isolationism | alliance |

How does a young nation become powerful? How does it grow larger?
Read this selection to learn how the United States became a world power.

Becoming a World Power

The United States grew until it reached the Pacific Ocean. Then people began to think about new ways of growing. They were in favor of imperialism. **Imperialism** is the practice of one country taking over a smaller or weaker country. For example, in 1898, the United States took over Hawaii.

How does this picture illustrate American imperialism?

The Spanish-American War

The United States also got land by going to war. At the end of the 1800s, Spain ruled Cuba. The Cuban people wanted to be free. They started a revolt against Spain. A **revolt** is a violent action by people against their ruler. Many Americans wanted to help the Cubans with their revolt. But Americans who had invested money in Cuban businesses wanted the United States to help Spain. To **invest** is to put money in a business deal to make a profit.

When an American ship sank in Cuba, the United States blamed Spain. In 1898, it declared war on Spain.

Spain also controlled the Philippine Islands, in Asia. The United States fought in the war there as well as in Cuba. Guerrillas from the Philippines helped the Americans. A **guerrilla** is a person who carries out surprise attacks.

The biggest battle of the Spanish-American War took place in Cuba. On July 1, 1898, the **cavalry**, soldiers on horseback, captured San Juan Hill. Spain could not hold on to Cuba.

The war was soon over. In 1899, the United States gained Puerto Rico and the Philippines. Cuba became a United States protectorate. A **protectorate** is a country that is protected and controlled by a stronger country.

The soldiers that captured San Juan Hill were known as the "Rough Riders."

The Panama Canal

The United States wanted to build a canal across Panama. At the time, Colombia ruled Panama. President Roosevelt tried to **negotiate** with Colombia to buy some land. But the country's leader did not want to talk about the matter to reach an agreement. Then Panama revolted against Colombia. Panama and the United States fought against Colombia and won. The new nation of Panama then let the United States build the canal.

Voices of Protest

Some people did not like the way that the United States had gained power. They favored **isolationism**. They wanted to stay out of the politics and business of other countries. They did not want to fight in **foreign** wars, wars outside the country. They also did not want to join the alliances forming in Europe. An **alliance** is a group of countries with a common purpose. Alliances helped lead to World War I.

The Panama Canal

United States

Atlantic Ocean

Pacific Ocean

Colombia

South America

Country of Panama

Panama Canal

My Social Studies Vocabulary

Go to page 96 to list other words you have learned about how the United States became a world power.

Becoming a World Power

imperialism   invest   cavalry   negotiate   foreign
revolt   guerrilla   protectorate   isolationism   alliance

A.   *Fill in the blanks with the correct vocabulary word.*

1.   soldiers on horseback

     __ __ __ __ __ __ __

2.   a weaker country or land under the control of a stronger one

     __ __ __ __ __ __ __ __ __ __ __ __

3.   a fighter who sneaks up on the enemy

     __ __ __ __ __ __ __ __ __

4.   a violent action by people against their ruler

     __ __ __ __ __ __

5.   the practice of one country taking over a smaller or weaker country

     __ __ __ __ __ __ __ __ __ __ __

6.   to put money in a business deal to make a profit

     __ __ __ __ __ __

7.   outside of a country

     __ __ __ __ __ __ __

8.   a policy of staying out of other countries' affairs

     __ __ __ __ __ __ __ __ __ __ __ __

9.   to talk about something to reach an agreement

     __ __ __ __ __ __ __ __ __

10.   a group of countries that joins together for common purposes

     __ __ __ __ __ __ __ __

Becoming a World Power

| imperialism | invest | cavalry | negotiate | foreign |
| revolt | guerrilla | protectorate | isolationism | alliance |

B. *Circle the word that makes sense in each sentence. Then write the word.*

1. The angry people of Cuba started a (cavalry, revolt) against their rulers.

   _____

2. If you (invest, revolt) money, you want to make money.

   _____

3. Several countries in Europe joined together to form the (alliance, protectorate).

   _____

4. Members of the (cavalry, protectorate) followed their leaders to victory in Cuba.

   _____

5. Fighting a war in a (guerrilla, foreign) country could cost a lot of money.

   _____

6. It was hard to fight against the (alliance, guerrilla) who snuck up on the
   enemy. _____

7. People who wanted the United States to mind its own business favored
   (imperialism, isolationism). _____

8. The ruler of Colombia was not willing to (invest, negotiate) to reach
   an agreement. _____

9. The United States made some of the laws for the (guerrilla, protectorate).

   _____

10. The United States became a world power through (imperialism, isolationism).

    _____

WORD ROOT

The word **isolationism** comes from
the Latin root **insula**, meaning "island."

Becoming a World Power

| imperialism | invest | cavalry | negotiate | foreign |
| revolt | guerrilla | protectorate | isolationism | alliance |

C. *Choose the correct vocabulary word to complete each sentence.*

1. The United States became more powerful through _____ .

2. People who wanted the United States to stay out of world affairs believed in

   _____ .

3. The nations had many of the same interests so they formed an

   _____ .

4. The Battle of San Juan Hill was fought by soldiers in the

   _____ .

5. People who believed in isolationism did not want Americans to be involved in

   _____ wars.

6. The United States looked after its _____ .

7. The troops were surprised by the attack of the _____ .

8. If a country's ruler refuses to talk, you cannot _____

   with him.

9. Cubans who disliked their Spanish rulers joined in the

   _____ .

10. A person who had decided to _____ in Cuba wanted

    the United States to side with Spain.

| imperialism | invest | cavalry | negotiate | foreign |
| revolt | guerrilla | protectorate | isolationism | alliance |

D. *Use each word in a sentence that shows you know the meaning of the word.*

1. foreign _____

_____

2. negotiate _____

_____

3. protectorate _____

_____

4. isolationism _____

_____

5. invest _____

_____

6. alliance _____

_____

7. imperialism _____

_____

8. cavalry _____

_____

9. guerrilla_____

_____

10. revolt _____

_____

Write!

Write your response to the prompt on a separate sheet of paper.
Use as many vocabulary words as you can in your writing.

Imagine that you live in 1907. How do you feel about the United States becoming a world power? State your opinion and explain it.

LESSON 15

combat	trench warfare	stalemate	slogan	casualties
diplomacy	front	propaganda	mobilization	reparations

In the summer of 1914, World War I began in Europe. Why would the United States want to stay out of the war at first? Why would it eventually decide to join in? Read this selection to learn why the United States finally entered World War I.

World War I

By 1907, Europe was split into two sides. Austria-Hungary, Germany, and Italy were on one side. Great Britain, France, and Russia were on the other side. Each side built up weapons and large armies. Each side was ready for **combat**, or armed fighting. Americans did not want to take sides. They hoped that diplomacy would win out. **Diplomacy** is the making of peaceful agreements between nations.

However, in 1914, a member of the royal family of Austria-Hungary was shot. World War I began.

New Ways of Fighting

World War I was a bloody and awful war. One reason was new war machines, such as tanks and airplanes. Another reason was trench warfare. In **trench warfare**, soldiers fire guns at one another from ditches, or trenches, dug in the ground.

Soldiers dug trenches in the ground.

In World War I, soldiers on the front mainly stayed in the trenches. A **front** is the place where the fighting is going on.

Trench warfare made it hard for either side to win the war. The front often stayed in the same place for months at a time. This was a **stalemate**, a state of no progress or change. The two sides were dug into the ground, and neither side could move. The war dragged on.

The United States Enters the War

Many Americans wanted to stay out of the war. Then Germany sank a British ship with many American passengers. Some Americans began to change their minds.

The United States government used propaganda to change more people's minds. **Propaganda** is anything used to influence people's thinking or actions. Propaganda often uses signs and slogans. A **slogan** is a short saying. It is easy to remember.

The United States entered the war in 1917. The government faced the huge job of mobilization. **Mobilization** is the raising, training, and supplying of an army. Thousands of American soldiers were sent to Europe. The United States, Great Britain, France, and other nations won the war.

The War Ends

The war ended in 1918. The costs of the war were very high. There were about 42 million casualties. **Casualties** are the dead and wounded. World War I was such a huge war, it was called "the war to end all wars."

Germany was one of the nations that lost the war. After the war, Germany was not allowed to have an army. It also had to pay reparations to Great Britain, France, and other nations. **Reparations** are payments for damages made by a defeated nation in war. Reparations left Germany poor and bitter. In 1939, Germany would be at war in Europe again.

These World War I posters were pro-war propaganda.

My Social Studies Vocabulary

Go to page 98 to list other words you have learned about World War I.

| combat | trench warfare | stalemate | slogan | casualties |
| diplomacy | front | propaganda | mobilization | reparations |

A. *Choose the word that best answers each question.*

1. I am the place where the fighting is going on. What am I?

   mobilization   slogan   front

2. We are payments for damages by a defeated nation in war. What are we?

   casualties   reparations   diplomacy

3. I am a kind of fighting that takes place from ditches. What am I?

   trench warfare   combat   propaganda

4. I am a short saying that is easy to remember. What am I?

   stalemate   front   slogan

5. We are the wounded and the dead. Who are we?

   propaganda   reparations   casualties

6. I am a state of no progress or change. What am I?

   front   stalemate   combat

7. I am the raising, training, and supplying of an army. What am I?

   mobilization   trench warfare   stalemate

8. I am fighting. What am I?

   combat   casualties   slogan

9. I make peaceful agreements between nations. What am I?

   mobilization   diplomacy   trench warfare

10. I am anything used to influence people's thinking or actions. What am I?

    propaganda   front   reparations

| combat | trench warfare | stalemate | slogan | casualties |
| diplomacy | front | propaganda | mobilization | reparations |

B. *Choose and write the two words that best complete each sentence.*

reparations	front	mobilization	casualties

1. Although Germany had to pay _____ , it could never

   make up for the suffering caused by millions of _____ .

trench warfare	combat	slogan	propaganda

2. A new form of _____ in World War I was called

   _____ .

combat	propaganda	slogan	reparations

3. The _____ was a form of _____ that

   the government used to persuade people to support the war.

mobilization	diplomacy	trench warfare	stalemate

4. Even though the fighting was at a _____ , the

   _____ of troops had to continue.

diplomacy	reparations	stalemate	front

5. Some Americans preferred _____ to sending United States

   soldiers to the _____ .

WORD ROOT

The word **combat** comes from the Latin word **battere**, meaning "to beat."

| combat | trench warfare | stalemate | slogan | casualties |
| diplomacy | front | propaganda | mobilization | reparations |

C. *Choose the correct vocabulary word to complete each sentence.*

1. "Be all you can be" is an example of a _____ .

2. The natural disaster resulted in a large number of _____ .

3. Great Britain received _____ from Germany after World War I.

4. The United States hoped that _____ would avoid a war.

5. After the United States declared war, the _____ of troops increased.

6. Soldiers who took part in _____ fought from ditches.

7. The armies were trained and ready for _____ .

8. Both sides wanted to end the _____ and to start making progress.

9. Soldiers often lose their lives at the _____ .

10. Some people were convinced to fight by posters and other _____ .

| combat | trench warfare | stalemate | slogan | casualties |
| diplomacy | front | propaganda | mobilization | reparations |

D. *Use each word in a sentence that shows you know the meaning of the word.*

1. stalemate _____

_____

2. combat _____

_____

3. casualties _____

_____

4. slogan _____

_____

5. diplomacy _____

_____

6. trench warfare _____

_____

7. propaganda _____

_____

8. reparations _____

_____

9. mobilization _____

_____

10. front _____

_____

Write!

Write your response to the prompt on a separate sheet of paper.
Use as many vocabulary words as you can in your writing.

Imagine that you are a soldier fighting in the trenches in World War I.
Tell some of your thoughts and feelings about the war.

My Social Studies Vocabulary

Lesson 1: The Break from Great Britain

_____ _____ _____

_____ _____ _____

_____ _____ _____

_____ _____ _____

_____ _____ _____

Lesson 2: The Roots of the Constitution

_____ _____ _____

_____ _____ _____

_____ _____ _____

_____ _____ _____

Lesson 3: The Constitution

_____ _____ _____

_____ _____ _____

_____ _____ _____

_____ _____ _____

Lesson 4: The Early Years of the United States

_____ _____ _____

_____ _____ _____

_____ _____ _____

_____ _____ _____

Lesson 5: The New Nation and the World

_____ _____ _____

_____ _____ _____

_____ _____ _____

_____ _____ _____

Lesson 6: Settling the West

_____ _____ _____

_____ _____ _____

_____ _____ _____

_____ _____ _____

Lesson 7: An Expanding Nation

_____   _____   _____

_____   _____   _____

_____   _____   _____

_____   _____   _____

_____   _____   _____

Lesson 8: The Road to War

_____   _____   _____

_____   _____   _____

_____   _____   _____

_____   _____   _____

_____   _____   _____

Lesson 9: The Civil War

_____   _____   _____

_____   _____   _____

_____   _____   _____

_____   _____   _____

_____   _____   _____

My Social Studies Vocabulary

Lesson 10: Reconstruction

_____ _____ _____

_____ _____ _____

_____ _____ _____

_____ _____ _____

_____ _____ _____

Lesson 11: Industrialization

_____ _____ _____

_____ _____ _____

_____ _____ _____

_____ _____ _____

_____ _____ _____

Lesson 12: The Growth of Cities

_____ _____ _____

_____ _____ _____

_____ _____ _____

_____ _____ _____

_____ _____ _____

Lesson 13: The Age of Reform

_____   _____   _____

_____   _____   _____

_____   _____   _____

_____   _____   _____

_____   _____   _____

Lesson 14: Becoming a World Power

_____   _____   _____

_____   _____   _____

_____   _____   _____

_____   _____   _____

_____   _____   _____

Lesson 15: World War I

_____   _____   _____

_____   _____   _____

_____   _____   _____

_____   _____   _____

_____   _____   _____

My Social Studies Vocabulary

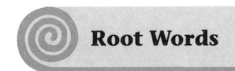

Root Words

A word that is the beginning, or source, of a new word is called a "root word." Many English words have roots in other languages. Latin and Greek are two languages that have given English many new words. The study of history is rich in words that come to English from these languages. The word *history* itself comes from a Latin word *historia*, which means "story" or "tale."

This chart shows some Latin and Greek roots, their meanings, and examples of English words that use the roots. Use the space provided to write other words with the same roots and to add new roots, meanings, and examples.

Latin or Greek Root	Meaning	Examples
terra	land	territory, _____ , _____ , _____
urb	city	urbanization, _____ , _____ , _____
emendare	fix	amendment, _____ , _____ , _____
_____	_____	_____ , _____
_____	_____	_____ , _____
_____	_____	_____ , _____
_____	_____	_____ , _____
_____	_____	_____ , _____

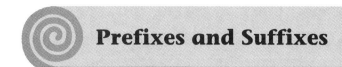

Prefixes and Suffixes

Prefixes

A prefix is one or more letters or syllables added to the beginning of a word to change the meaning. For example, *pre-* is a prefix that means "before." Think of the word *cook*, which means "to prepare food." If you add the prefix *pre-* to *cook*, the new word *precook* means "to cook before."

Prefix	Meaning	Examples
mono-	single, alone	monopoly, _____ , _____
in-	not	independence, _____ , _____
ex-	out of	expansion, _____ , _____
_____	_____	_____ , _____ , _____
_____	_____	_____ , _____ , _____

Suffixes

A suffix is one or more letters added to the end of a word. Some suffixes make a noun plural (*-s* added to *rock* becomes *rocks*) or change the tense of a verb (*-ed* added to *jump* becomes *jumped*). Other suffixes change the meaning of the word. For example, *-hood* is a suffix that means "the state of." If you add it to the word *child*, the new word *childhood* means "the state of being a child."

Suffix	Meaning	Examples
-ist	a person who believes	abolitionist, _____ , _____
-cracy	rule	democracy, _____ , _____
-ism	a state of ideas, a practice	sectionalism, _____ , _____
_____	_____	_____ , _____ , _____
_____	_____	_____ , _____ , _____

Glossary

Aa

abolish (uh-BOL-ihsh)
to put an end to something
(Lesson 8, page 46)

abolitionist
(ab-uh-LIHSH-uh-nihst)
a person who worked to end
slavery
(Lesson 8, page 46)

adjoining (uh-JOY-nihng)
next to
(Lesson 6, page 34)

administration (ad-mihn-uh-STRAY-shuhn)
a president's time in office
(Lesson 4, page 22)

alliance (uh-LY-uhns)
a group of nations that join together
for a common purpose
(Lesson 14, page 83)

amendment (uh-MEHND-muhnt)
a change to a document, such as the
Constitution of the United States
(Lesson 3, page 17)

annex (ah-NEHKS)
to add to something larger
or more important
(Lesson 7, page 41)

armistice (AHR-muh-stihs)
an agreement to stop fighting
(Lesson 5, page 29)

assassination
(uh-sas-uh-NAY-shuhn)
the killing of a
public figure
(Lesson 10, page 58)

authority (uh-THAWR-uh-tee)
official power
(Lesson 1, page 4)

Bb

black codes (blak kohdz)
laws that limited the rights of freedmen
(Lesson 10, page 59)

blockade (blo-KAYD)
to prevent ships from entering or leaving
a port
(Lesson 5, page 28)

boom (boom)
a sudden increase
(Lesson 8, page 46)

boundary (BOWN-duhr-ee)
a border
(Lesson 7, page 40)

Cc

cabinet (KAB-uh-niht)
the group of people
who give advice to the
United States president
and make up the heads
of departments
(Lesson 4, page 22)

canal (kuh-NAL)
a manmade
waterway that
connects
two bodies of
water
(*Lesson 6, page 35*)

capitalism (KAP-uh-tuh-lihz-uhm)
a system in which privately owned
businesses control production
(*Lesson 7, page 41*)

carpetbagger
(KAHR-piht-bag-uhr)
a Northerner who went
to the South during
Reconstruction
(*Lesson 10, page 59*)

casualties (KAZH-u-uhl-teez)
people who are killed or wounded
(*Lesson 15, page 89*)

cavalry (KAV-uhl-ree)
soldiers on horseback
(*Lesson 14, page 83*)

checks and balances
(chehks and BAL-uhns-ihz)
a system in which each branch of
government can limit the actions
of the other branches
(*Lesson 3, page 17*)

civil war (SIHV-uhl wawr)
a war between groups in the same country
(*Lesson 9, page 52*)

clause (klawz)
a section of a piece of legal writing
(*Lesson 1, page 5*)

colony (KOL-uh-nee)
an area ruled by another
country
(*Lesson 1, page 4*)

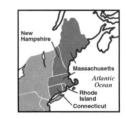

combat (KOM-bat)
armed fighting
(*Lesson 15, page 88*)

commute (kuh-MYOOT)
the trip to and from
one's home to a job
(*Lesson 12, page 71*)

compact (KOM-pakt)
an agreement
(*Lesson 2, page 11*)

compromise (KOM-pruh-myz)
a way of settling a disagreement in which
each side gives up something
(*Lesson 3, page 16*)

conductor (kuhn-DUHK-tuhr)
a person who led a group
of slaves to freedom on the
Underground Railroad
(*Lesson 8, page 47*)

Confederacy (kuhn-FEHD-uhr-uh-see)
the group of Southern states that left
the nation
(*Lesson 9, page 52*)

confederation (kuhn-fehd-uh-RAY-shuhn)
a group of independent states that
work together
(*Lesson 3, page 16*)

constitution (kon-stuh-TOO-shuhn)
a set of laws and ideas that describe
how a government works
(Lesson 2, page 10)

controversy (KON-truh-vur-see)
public disagreement between two sides
with opposite views
(Lesson 4, page 23)

convention (kuhn-VEHN-shuhn)
a meeting
for a
particular
purpose
*(Lesson 3,
page 16)*

corporation (kawr-puh-RAY-shuhn)
a business owned by many people each of
whom own a share, or part, of the business
(Lesson 11, page 65)

corruption (kuh-RUHP-shuhn)
a lack of honesty
(Lesson 13, page 77)

Dd

declaration
(dehk-luh-RAY-shuhn)
a serious statement
about something
(Lesson 1, page 5)

defensive
(dih-FEHN-sihv)
done to protect against attack
(Lesson 9, page 52)

delegates (DEHL-uh-gihtz)
people chosen to speak and vote for a group
(Lesson 3, page 16)

democracy (dih-MOK-ruh-see)
a system of government run by the people
who live under it
(Lesson 3, page 17)

diplomacy (duh-PLOH-muh-see)
the making of peaceful agreements
among nations
(Lesson 15, page 88)

doctrine (DOK-truhn)
a statement of government policy
(Lesson 5, page 29)

document (DOK-yuh-muhnt)
a formal piece of writing
(Lesson 2, page 11)

draft (draft)
to choose someone from a group
to serve in the armed forces
(Lesson 9, page 53)

Ee

economy (ih-KON-uh-mee)
all the business activities of a country or state
(Lesson 7, page 41)

emancipation
(ih-man-suh-PAY-shuhn)
the act of setting people
free
(Lesson 9, page 53)

embargo (ehm-BAHR-goh)
a ban on goods leaving a country
(Lesson 5, page 28)

emigration (ehm-uh-GRAY-shuhn)
the leaving of one's country to live
in another
(Lesson 12, page 70)

entrepreneur (ahn-truh-pruh-NUR)
someone who starts a business, taking
all the risks but getting all the profit
(Lesson 7, page 41)

ethnic group (EHTH-nihk groop)
people related by customs, language,
culture, or country of origin
(Lesson 12, page 71)

excise tax (EHK-syz taks)
money paid to the government
by a maker or seller of a product
(Lesson 4, page 23)

executive branch
(ehg-ZEHK-yuh-tihv brahnch)
the part of the government
that carries out laws
(Lesson 4, page 22)

expansion (ehk-SPAN-shuhn)
an increase in size
(Lesson 7, page 40)

Ff

federalism (FEHD-uhr-uh-lihz-uhm)
a system in which state and national
governments share power and duties
(Lesson 3, page 17)

foreign (FAWR-uhn)
outside one's own country
(Lesson 14, page 83)

foundation (fown-DAY-shun)
the base upon which something is built
(Lesson 2, page 10)

freedmen (FREED-muhn)
former slaves
(Lesson 10, page 58)

freight (frayt)
goods carried by a
ship, truck, train,
or airplane
(Lesson 6, page 35)

front (fruhnt)
a place where the fighting in a war
is going on
(Lesson 15, page 88)

frontier (fruhn-TIHR)
an area of few people at the edge
of a settled area
(Lesson 6, page 34)

fugitive (FYOO-juh-tihv)
a runaway
(Lesson 8, page 47)

Gg

Great Awakening (grayt uh-WAY-kuh-ning)
a period in the early 1700s of renewed
interest in religion
(Lesson 1, page 4)

guerrilla (guh-RIHL-uh)
a person who carries out surprise attacks
(Lesson 14, page 83)

Hh

homeland (HOHM-land)
the land that a person comes from
(Lesson 6, page 35)

Ii

immigrant
(IHM-uh-gruhnt)
a person who comes to
a new country to live
(Lesson 12, page 70)

imperialism (ihm-PIHR-ee-uh-lihz-uhm)
the practice of one country taking over
a smaller or weaker country
(Lesson 14, page 82)

impress (ihm-PREHS)
to force a person into
military service
(Lesson 5, page 28)

independence (ihn-dih-PEHN-duhns)
freedom from control
(Lesson 1, page 5)

industrialization
(ihn-duhs-tree-uh-luh-ZAY-shuhn)
the change from farming to industry
(Lesson 11, page 64)

inherit (ihn-HEHR-iht)
to get something from someone after
he or she has died
(Lesson 10, page 59)

invention (ihn-VEHN-shuhn)
an original idea for a new process or product
(Lesson 11, page 64)

invest (ihn-VEHST)
to put money into a business deal
to make a profit
(Lesson 14, page 82)

isolationism (y-suh-LAY-shuh-nihz-uhm)
the belief in staying out of the business
and politics of other countries
(Lesson 14, page 83)

Jj

Jim Crow laws (jhim kroh lawz)
laws that separated African Americans
and whites in public places
(Lesson 13, page 76)

Kk

kickback (KIHK-bak)
a payment to a person who controls
a source of money
(Lesson 13, page 77)

Ll

labor union (LAY-buhr YOON-yuhn)
a group of workers who join together
to bring changes
(Lesson 11, page 65)

land grant (land grant)
public land given by a government
(Lesson 7, page 41)

landslide (LAND-slyd)
the winning of an election by a very large
majority of votes
(Lesson 5, page 29)

latitude (LAT-uh-tood)
the distance on Earth north or south
of the equator
(Lesson 7, page 40)

literacy test (LIHT-uhr-uh-see tehst)
a test that checks a person's ability
to read and write
(Lesson 13, page 76)

Mm

Magna Carta (MAG-nuh KAHR-tuh)
a list of political rights signed by
the king of England in 1215
(Lesson 2, page 10)

Manifest Destiny
(MAN-uh-fehst DEHS-tuh-nee)
the belief that the United States had
the right to extend its boundaries from
the Atlantic Ocean to the Pacific Ocean
(Lesson 7, page 40)

mass production
(mas pruh-DUHK-shuhn)
the process of making
things in large amounts,
usually by machine
(Lesson 7, page 41)

mobilization (moh-buh-luh-ZAY-shuhn)
the raising, training, and supplying
of an army
(Lesson 15, page 89)

monarchy (MON-uhr-kee)
rule by one person, such as a king or queen
(Lesson 2, page 11)

monopoly (muh-NOP-uh-lee)
a company that controls an industry or
business by getting rid of all its competition
(Lesson 11, page 65)

muckraker (MUHK-ray-kuhr)
a writer who reveals dishonest
or unfair practices
(Lesson 13, page 77)

Glossary

Nn

nationalism (NASH-uh-nuh-lihz-uhm)
pride in one's country
(Lesson 5, page 29)

nativism (NAY-tuh-vihz-uhm)
the practice or policy of favoring native-born
people over immigrants
(Lesson 12, page 70)

negotiate (nih-GOH-shee-ayt)
to discuss a matter to reach an agreement
(Lesson 14, page 83)

neutrality (noo-TRAL-uh-tee)
a policy of not taking sides during a war
(Lesson 4, page 23)

Oo

opportunity (op-uhr-TOO-nuh-tee)
a chance to make money or to better oneself
(Lesson 6, page 34)

ordinance (AWR-duh-nuhns)
a rule or law
(Lesson 6, page 35)

Pp

panic (PAN-ihk)
a time when businesses fail, jobs disappear,
and banks close
(Lesson 11, page 65)

parliament (PAHR-luh-mehnt)
a group of people chosen to make laws
(Lesson 2, page 10)

pilgrim (PIHL-gruhm)
a person who travels a long distance for
religious reasons
(Lesson 2, page 11)

pioneer (py-uh-NIHR)
one of the first people
to settle an area
(Lesson 6, page 34)

policy (POL-uh-see)
a plan of action
(Lesson 4, page 23)

political (puh-LIHT-uh-kuhl)
having to do with the government
(Lesson 1, page 4)

political machine
(puh-LIHT-uh-kuhl muh-SHEEN)
an organized group of people in government
with power
(Lesson 13, page 77)

poll tax (pohl taks)
money that must be paid in order to vote
(Lesson 13, page 76)

preach (preech)
to talk about religious subjects
(Lesson 1, page 4)

propaganda
(prop-uh-GAN-duh)
anything used to influence
people's thinking or actions
(Lesson 15, page 89)

protectorate (pruh-TEHK-tuhr-iht)

a country that is protected and controlled by a stronger country

(Lesson 14, page 83)

Rr

radical (RAD-uh-kuhl)

a person who is in favor of extreme changes

(Lesson 8, page 47)

Reconstruction (ree-kuhn-STRUHK-shuhn)

the plan to rebuild the South and bring it back into the United States

(Lesson 10, page 58)

reformer (rih-FAWR-muhr)

a person who works for change for the better

(Lesson 13, page 77)

regulate (REHG-yuh-layt)

to control

(Lesson 11, page 65)

reparations (rehp-uh-RAY-shuhns)

payments for damages made by a defeated nation in war

(Lesson 15, page 89)

reserved powers (rih-ZURVD POW-uhrz)

powers given to the states

(Lesson 3, page 17)

revenue (REHV-uh-noo)

income that a government collects to pay for public expenses

(Lesson 4, page 23)

revolt (rih-VOHLT)

a violent action of people against their ruler

(Lesson 14, page 82)

revolution (rehv-uh-LOO-shuhn)

a war against one's own government

(Lesson 1, page 5)

rights (ryts)

freedoms owed to people

(Lesson 1, page 5)

riot (RY-uht)

a crowd of people who become out of control

(Lesson 9, page 53)

Ss

scalawag (SKAL-uh-wag)

a Southern white person who was in favor of Reconstruction

(Lesson 10, page 59)

secede (sih-SEED)

to withdraw from a country to form a new country

(Lesson 8, page 47)

sectionalism (SEHK-shuh-nuh-lihz-uhm)
loyalty to one's region rather than the
whole country
(Lesson 8, page 47)

segregation
(sehg-ruh-GAY-shuhn)
the practice of separating
people by race
(Lesson 10, page 59)

separation of powers
(sehp-uh-RAY-shuhn uhv POW-uhrz)
the separation of the government into
three branches
(Lesson 3, page 17)

settlement house (SEHT-uhl-muhnt hows)
a place that offers services to help
poor people
(Lesson 13, page 77)

sharecropper
(SHAIR-krop-uhr)
a farmer who works
someone else's land in
return for a share of
the crop
(Lesson 10, page 58)

skyscraper (SKY-skray-puhr)
a very tall building
(Lesson 12, page 71)

slogan (SLOH-guhn)
a short saying that is easy to remember
(Lesson 15, page 89)

slum (sluhm)
a poor, crowded
part of a city
(Lesson 12, page 71)

spoils system (spoylz SIHS-tuhm)
the practice of giving government jobs
to supporters
(Lesson 5, page 29)

stalemate (STAYL-mayt)
a state of no progress or change
(Lesson 15, page 89)

strike (stryk)
stopping work to try to get higher pay or
better working conditions
(Lesson 11, page 65)

subject (SUHB-jehkt)
under the power of another
(Lesson 2, page 11)

suburb (SUHB-uhrb)
an area just beyond the city limits
(Lesson 12, page 71)

sue (soo)
to bring legal action to settle a dispute
(Lesson 8, page 47)

suffrage (SUHF-rihj)
the right to vote
(Lesson 13, page 77)

surrender (suh-REHN-duhr)
to declare that an enemy has won and that
fighting can stop
(Lesson 9, page 53)

sweatshop
(SWEHT-shop)
a small factory or
mill with poor
working conditions
(*Lesson 11, page 65*)

Tt ─────────────────

tariff (TAR-ihf)
a tax on goods brought into a country
(*Lesson 4, page 23*)

taxation (tak-SAY-shuhn)
the system of paying taxes, or money paid to
support the government
(*Lesson 2, page 11*)

technology (tehk-NOL-uh-jee)
the use of scientific knowledge to make
machines and tools
(*Lesson 6, page 35*)

tenant farmer (TEHN-uhnt FAHR-muhr)
a farmer who pays rent to work someone
else's land
(*Lesson 10, page 58*)

tenement (TEHN-uh-muhnt)
a crowded apartment building
(*Lesson 12, page 71*)

territory (TEHR-uh-tawr-ee)
land under control of a country
(*Lesson 5, page 29*)

total war (TOH-tuhl wawr)
the practice of attacking the enemy's
civilians and resources, as well as the army
(*Lesson 9, page 53*)

transcontinental
(trans-kon-tuh-NEHN-tuhl)
going across the continent
(*Lesson 11, page 64*)

treasury (TREHZH-uhr-ee)
the department in charge of collecting taxes
and managing public funds
(*Lesson 4, page 22*)

trench warfare (trehnch WAWR-fair)
fighting from or across long, narrow ditches
dug in the ground
(*Lesson 15, page 88*)

turning point (TUR-nihng poynt)
a major change of direction
(*Lesson 9, page 53*)

turnpike (TURN-pyk)
a road that
travelers have to
pay to use
(*Lesson 6, page 35*)

Uu

Underground Railroad
(UHN-duhr-grownd RAYL-rohd)
a system of people who helped slaves
to escape from the South
(Lesson 8, page 47)

Union (YOON-yuhn)
the nation, or the Northern states,
after the South left the nation
(Lesson 9, page 52)

urbanization (ur-buh-nuh-ZAY-shuhn)
the growth of cities
(Lesson 12, page 70)

Vv

veto (VEE-toh)
to vote "no"
(Lesson 5, page 29)

Acknowledgments

Developer: Maureen Devine Sotoohi
Writer: DeVona Dors
Cover Design: Susan Hawk
Designer: Pat Lucas
Photo Credits:
Front Cover: clockwise from top left James Steidl/
Shutterstock.com; The Granger Collection,
New York; Library of Congress, Prints &
Photographs Division, LC-DIG-ppmsca-13484;
©Bettmann/CORBIS

p. 4   Copyright ©North Wind/North Wind Picture
Archives

p. 5   (top, bottom) ©2007 JupiterImages Corporation

p. 10   Cassell's History of England/Wikipedia.org

p. 11   (top, bottom) The Granger Collection, New York

p. 16   ©Bettmann/CORBIS

p. 22   National Archives

p. 23   (left) Library of Congress, Thomas Jefferson
Papers Collection, 3g02474b, National Archives;
(right) The Granger Collection, New York

p. 28   ©2007 JupiterImages Corporation

p. 29   (top) Allyn Cox/Architect of the Capitol/Capitol
Complex; (bottom) Library of Congress, Prints &
Photographs Division, LC-USZC4-6221

p. 35   (left) Library of Congress, Prints & Photographs
Division, LC-Z62-110382; (right) The Granger
Collection, New York

p. 46   ©Bettmann/CORBIS

p. 47   Louis Schultze/Wikipedia.org

p. 53   (left top) ©2007 JupiterImages Corporation;
(left bottom) Library of Congress, Prints &
Photographs Division, LC-DIG-ppmsca-13484;
(right) Library of Congress, Prints & Photographs
Division, LC-DIG-pga-03235

p. 58   Library of Congress, Prints & Photographs
Division, LC-USF34-017965-C

p. 59   Library of Congress, Prints & Photographs
Division, LC-USZ62-77793

p. 64   National Archives

p. 65   (top) Library of Congress, Prints & Photographs
Division, LC-USZC4-435; (bottom) ©Bettmann/
CORBIS

p. 70   Library of Congress, Prints & Photographs
Division, LOT-11687-5

p. 71   (top) ©Bettmann/CORBIS; (bottom) CORBIS

p. 76   Thomas D. McAvoy/Stringer/Time & Life Pictures/
Getty Images

p. 77   (top) ©Bettmann/CORBIS; (bottom) Library of
Congress, Prints & Photographs Division,
LC-DIG-ggbain-0078

p. 82   The Granger Collection, New York

p. 83   ©Bettmann/CORBIS

p. 88   National Archives

p. 89   (top, bottom) Library of Congress, Prints &
Photographs Division, LC-USZC4-3859;
LC-USZ62-4215064

p. 101 (abolitionist) Courtesy of Texas Portrait Gallery;
(assassination) Library of Congress, Prints &
Photographs Division, LC-USZC2-1947; (cabinet)
National Archives

p. 102 (canal) Evergreene Painting Studio/Architect of
the Capitol; (carpetbagger) Library of Congress,
Prints & Photographs Division, LC-USZ62-77793;
(commute) Natalia Bratslavsky/Shutterstock.
com; (conductor) Library of Congress, Prints &
Photographs Division, LC-USZ62-5816

p. 103 (convention) ©Bettmann/CORBIS; (declaration)
©Corbis; (emancipation) ©2007 JupiterImages
Corporation

p. 104 (executive branch) Ken Hammond/USDA Photo
Library; (freight) Anyka/Shutterstock.com

p. 105 (immigrant) National Archives; (impress) ©2007
JupiterImages Corporation

p. 106 (mass production) ©2007 JupiterImages
Corporation; (muckraker) Library of Congress,
Prints & Photographs Division, LC-DIG-ggbain-
0078

p. 107 (pioneer) ©2007 JupiterImages Corporation;
(propaganda) Library of Congress, Prints &
Photographs Division, LC-USZ62-4215064

p. 108 (Reconstruction) National Archives; (riot) ©Corbis

p. 109 (segregation) ©Bettmann/CORBIS; (sharecropper)
Library of Congress, Prints & Photographs
Division, LC-USF34-017965-C; (slum) Library of
Congress, Prints & Photographs Division,
LC-G612-T-46078

p. 110 (sweatshop) Library of Congress, Chicago Daily
News Collection, DN-0002416; (turnpike) U.S.
Department of Transportation

Illustration Credits:
pp. 34, 40, 41, 47, 52, 83, 102 (colony) Pat Lucas